LAFCADIO HEARN

By ARTHUR E. KUNST

University of Wisconsin

 158

Twayne Publishers, Inc.   ::   New York

Preface

LAFCADIO HEARN, who did not write on a large scale, has left behind no plays, no novels, and no narrative verse. The volumes of his collected works are composed of a vast number of small units: travel sketches, folklore, Gothic tales, impressions, and speculations. Such a wealth of materials inevitably presents problems to the critical student of Hearn the writer. Luckily, the scholarly groundwork on Hearn's fascinating and odd career has been done and done well by Albert Mordell, O. W. Frost, Elizabeth Stevenson, and Marcel Robert; besides this full biographical context, the nature of the writings themselves—personal experiences and personal obsessions—provides us with ample perspective on purpose and meaning.

I have tried to limit myself to Hearn's literary output, and, within that, to trace his development as a creative writer from his earliest days in Cincinnati to his last days in Japan. Because Hearn chose to work in some of the more perplexing and unusual literary forms, he raises critical issues that are interesting in themselves. It was impossible to appreciate his development without first trying to grasp the significance of his search for alternatives to plot, his passion for minute detail and shades of phrasing, and his insistence on the close relation of dream and nightmare to art. I have tried to fashion analytical tools that would do justice to the special virtues of Hearn's technique. But more than this, I have not sought only to discover the validity of his experiments but to explain why and where they failed. A close scrutiny of both success and failure is necessary to understand an author's development.

Given the extraordinary number of very small works (and, indeed, the manner in which these in turn are composed of fragments), I have tried to select for study those instances that signal Hearn's development or that most tellingly illustrate the possibilities of Hearn's style. A reader will find mention of nearly every one of Hearn's famous works, and, either in the discussion of it or of a closely related work, he should expect to find exposition of the most fruitful approaches to it.

One of the major problems of Lafcadio Hearn as a literary artist is that of the contribution of the translator. Readers are probably aware that Hearn spent many of his last years reshaping tales from the Japanese, but his work on the great nineteenth-century French writers is perhaps not well enough known. First of all, I have come to believe that in Hearn's translations lies the clue to a large part of his literary evolution; and second, a close consideration of the translations next to their originals shows how much Hearn added to them and made them his own. In the work of Lafcadio Hearn, the boundaries between translation and inspiration become useless and absurd.

Trying to isolate the critical problems of Hearn the literary man was, I felt, enough; and I have not dealt with his philosophical essays except in passing. Beongcheon Yu's study of Hearn as critic and thinker is, anyway, more than adequate in this respect. And since the present study limits itself to a concentrated analysis of the poetic and imaginative side of Hearn, the reader who is really curious about his work will be best off if he keeps a copy of Hearn close at hand.

Acknowledgments are extended to *Comparative Literature Studies* for permission to use material from the author's article "Lafcadio Hearn vis-à-vis French Literature" and to *Literature East and West,* for permission to use the author's article "Lafcadio Hearn's Use of Japanese Sources" (Vol. X, No. 3, pp. 245–63).

ARTHUR E. KUNST

University of Wisconsin

Chronology

1850   Patrick Lafcadio Hearn, born on the island of Lafcadio, off the west coast of Greece, to Charles Bush Hearn, officer in the British Army, and Rosa Cassimati, daughter of an old Ionian family.

1852–   In Dublin, Ireland. Mother goes insane, and is sent back
1863   to her home, 1854. Informal ward of a widowed, Roman Catholic great-aunt, Mrs. Brenane. Sent off to a seminary at Yvetot, France.

1863–   In school at St. Cuthbert's, Ushaw, in England. Blinded in
1868   left eye.

1868–   Abandoned by Mrs. Brenane. Some time in home of a
1869   former maid in London.

1869–   Arrival in America and settlement in Cincinnati, Ohio. Im-
1872   poverished.

1872–   On the Cincinnati *Enquirer*.
1875

1875–   On the Cincinnati *Commercial*.
1877

1877–   Trip down the Mississippi, and settlement in New Orleans.
1878   Impoverished.

1878–   Associate Editor of the New Orleans *Item*.
1881

1881–   On the New Orleans *Times-Democrat*.
1887

1882   *One of Cleopatra's Nights.*

1884   *Stray Leaves from Strange Literature.*

1885   Trip to Florida.

1887   *Some Chinese Ghosts.*

1887   In New York. First West Indian trip. Again in New York and environs.

1887–   In Martinique, French West Indies.
1889

1889   *Chita*. In Philadelphia.

1890   *The Crime of Sylvestre Bonnard. Two Years in the French West Indies. Youma.* "Karma." Voyage across Canada and the Pacific.

1890   Arrival in Japan at Yokohama.

1890–
1891   At Matsue, on the west coast of Honshū, as secondary school English teacher. Marries Setsu Koizumi, daughter of an old samurai family.

1891–
1894   At Kumamoto, on the island of Kyūshū, as teacher in another secondary school.

1894–
1895   At Kōbe, on the Inland Sea, as editor of the *Kobe Chronicle*.

1894   *Glimpses of Unfamiliar Japan.*

1895   *Out of the East.* Naturalized and adopted into the Koizumi family as Yakumo Koizumi.

1896   *Kokoro.*

1896–
1903   In Tōkyō, as lecturer on English Literature at the Imperial University.

1897   *Gleanings in Buddha-Fields.*

1898   *Exotics and Retrospectives.*

1899   *In Ghostly Japan.*

1900   *Shadowings.*

1901   *A Japanese Miscellany.*

1902   *Kottō.*

1903   Forced to resign from the university.

1904   Begins lectures at Waseda University. *Kwaidan.* Dies. *Japan: An Attempt at Interpretation.*

1905   *The Romance of the Milky Way.*

CHAPTER 1

Cincinnati

THE five years that young reporter Lafcadio Hearn spent in Cincinnati of the 1870's were an apprenticeship to his long career as journalist, traveler, and literary artist. His work for the *Enquirer* and the *Commercial* as a young reporter was essentially no different from the later interpretations and impressions of the West Indies and Japan through which he became famous. Not only was his ultimate development conditioned by his Cincinnati experience, but job requirements and talents certainly came together to let him find and prove what he could do well. For Hearn, the problem of journalism was the problem of combining honesty with art: the presentation of fact in a manner which was at the same time honest, compelling, and within the limits of artistic choice.

Those qualities which distinguish his later writings—a response to the outcasts of the world, an obsessive evocation of horror, a tendency to fragment experience into a stream of impressions, and, above all, a narrative personality which is subservient to the demands of his story—were all adopted in the Cincinnati years. These traits were well-suited to the demands of a city newspaper of the 1870's, but even then Hearn acquired a reputation for energy, for a finicky style, and for gory truthfulness. In order to achieve that reputation, as well as to leave the newspaper world behind him, Hearn apparently seized on the manifold opportunities that busy world provided him to find a literary method.

I   *On the Enquirer*

The earlier *Enquirer* years are dotted with newspaper stories in which Hearn is experimenting with his own possibilities. He is alternately hesitant or clumsy; his nervous sophistication obscures his subject, or his conscientious devotion to his notes leaves us with a bewildering sense of complete and aimless reality. He enters several promising paths, but fruitlessly—as if he were always being distracted by new temptations. He doesn't yet know what to do with himself, what to do with his language, or what to do with his information.

"John Algernon Owen" begins promisingly: "Mrs. M, the landlady of a boarding-house on a corner of Walnut and Ninth Streets, mourns the loss of two boarders, a man and wife, who softly stole out last Monday evening, leaving her nothing for an unpaid board-bill of $50 but a battered old trunk half-filled with manuscripts." [1] Several stories could have followed from the plaint of Mrs. M; the slippery career of the boarders, seen through the suspicious observations of their landlady; a sentimental exposé of the dreary house in which the vanished pair slowly exhausted their fund of unreasonable schemes; or a seesaw between the extravagant pretensions of the abandoned manuscripts and the seamy cynicism of their book of sales instructions. Hearn tries a little of all of them. So thorough is the research, and so fertile is the imaginative reconstruction of its meaning, that we are helpless to know whether any of the material is significant. The material for a vivid reality lies within his jumbled narrative; but at this stage—the first stage—it remains hidden.

"Almost a Riot" [2] is more modest, one story only: "Vine Street, last night, trembled on the edge of a riot. One blow of a policeman's club, and there would have been bloodshed." The scene is intended to be suspenseful, and the story never loses sight of that suspense. It starts with the assault, the gathering crowd; only the reputation of the hoodlum and the street are brought to bear from outside knowledge; and the motion does not stop until the bruised and torn officers breathe easy once again in the safety of the station.

What is wrong with the piece is essentially the language. It is an odd mixture of phrases bordering on slang; of lurching sentences; of borrowed, fashionable metaphors; and of neutral prose. Then Hearn writes: ". . . Eichelberger pulled out his club. At sight of this the crowd became furious. A mother defending her child could not have been more solicitous than these wretches for the safety of the body of the prisoner. Here was an excuse for an attack." [3] Embedded in this impersonal narrative is a comparison. First, its relevance is lessened by the eruption of upper-class words, "solicitous," and feelings, "wretches." Second, and more important, the comparison impedes the pace of the action.

Again and again with this *x: namely y* form of interruption, the focus of the reporting is turned round to the process of description. Language itself, rather than the thing described, becomes the standard by which the motion of the story is regulated. For example, we read: "At that second had Eichelberger touched the man with his club, it would have been the signal for an onslaught. It would have been the torch that would have set into flame the whole smoldering mass." [4] Then, unleashing the action again, "but he did not do it." The narrator sees the mob, sees the besieged policeman teetering on the edge of disaster, but—detrimental to the continuing excitement of the scene—he also sees his own prose. We become aware of him as narrator as well as point of view. And, as narrator, he has no living function in the tale.

By the time we reach his exposé entitled "Slow Starvation," [5] Hearn has discovered how to make himself a character in his own story. The process of investigation is brought under the scrutiny of the reader. Only the whole sense of indignation we might feel in the face of the poverty of the women who work at sewing is dispersed by the antics and posturings of the reporter sent to expose it. The facts are brought out, the reporter registers shock. Certainly Hearn captures the flavor of the interview—the brogue of the ruddy matron, the impromptu urgings of the interviewer:

'Yes. I want to know what prices are paid for the sewing.'
'Ah, the devil take the prices! Shure we don't get any prices at all now. I used to have a whole roomful of girls working for me; but since prices has come down, I haven't the face to offer them work for the little I could pay them. . . .'

Ogling the working girls and acting the buffoon, the narrative figure is concretely visible. What this self-conscious artistry now needs is a stage where visible narration is not an affront to the social uses of the description.

There are two ways out of this dilemma over the real participation of a journalist in the world Hearn will later try to re-create. One is to admit the world into one's inner life and to display all one's prejudices, fears, and greedy desires for inspection. Lafcadio Hearn tries time and again to take this path, but out of shame or embarrassment ends up creating the grotesque, some comical figure whose manner causes the reader to forget the suffering man inside. Only with the dream does Hearn evidently feel able to grapple publicly with his anxieties. Curiously, while he was in Cincinnati, not until his last piece, "Steeple Climbers," [6] does the frightened man, haunted by ghosts, come forward to acknowledge himself; and then he does so in a dreamlike experience of climbing which he also repeats later on Mount Pelée in Martinique and Mount Fuji in Japan.

Instead, Hearn chooses the second way out of an investigator's dilemma: as an artist he finds that he can make his subjects tell their history and reveal themselves in the telling. Our attention is called to their partiality by the very fact that they are not historians but characters. The real barbarity of the "Barbarous Barbers" [7] is not the racketeering and petty economies of their rivals: it is the garrulous monologues in which they gossip, accuse, and argue. The real "creditability" of the old slave's story in "Mr. Handy's Life" lies in the unevasive and unchanging neutrality in which the Negro recalls both desperation and floor-sweeping.

The unconscious hilarity of "The Cedar Closet" [8] only proves that, if Hearn wants to confront the supernatural, he must find a language which relates it to the world of Cincinnati: "In looking back, that time seems to me shadowed by a dark and terrible brooding cloud, bearing in its lurid gloom what, but for love and patience the tenderest and most untiring, might have been the bolt of death, or, worse a thousand times, of madness." [9]

We may compare this inherited, studied literary terror in the manner of Poe with Hearn's equally studied, but crudely valid evocation of human torture in the "Story of a Slave." [10] Both pieces try to let a woman narrate events she can scarcely stand to remember; but only the second tale utilizes a real woman. The section of "Story of a Slave" that is devoted to the whippings begins: "I worked under the meanest overseers, and got flogged and flogged, until I thought I should die." The slave woman doesn't remember with the appropriate, suggestive adjectives; she recalls her experience brutally, materially, in terms of leather, nails, wood: "They thought nothing of giving a woman three or four hundred blows with a long, heavy strap, made of harness leather, stuck full of tacks." And then, "The straps were fastened to short wooden handles." But this utter lack of emotional reaction from the narrating woman serves to make the scene starker and blacker: "At 4 o'clock she could not even scream, and would only shake and tremble when they struck her." The quietness of the interviewer is a tribute to the effect of the woman he is re-creating; he is not needed.

It would not be easy to say whether it was the usefulness of horror and sensation in selling newspapers or Hearn's natural taste for contemplating the bizarre that made him take so well to this type of subject, but there can be little doubt that the first and quickest success of his experiments came with the story "Violent Cremation." [11] The unusual bestiality of the crime—and Hearn's vivid mental exercise in recreating the act of stuffing a man into a furnace—had a sadistic appeal which is undeniable:

VIOLENT CREMATION
SATURDAY NIGHT'S HORRIBLE CRIME
A MAN MURDERED AND BURNED IN A FURNACE
THE TERRIBLE VENGEANCE OF A FATHER
ARREST OF THE SUPPOSED MURDERERS
LINKS OF CIRCUMSTANTIAL EVIDENCE
THE PITIFUL TESTIMONY OF A TREMBLING HORSE
SHOCKING DETAILS OF THE DIABOLISM
STATEMENTS AND CARTE DE VISITE OF THE ACCUSED

For the most part, this tale is familiar stuff, and Hearn's role is restricted to that of breathless fascination. But we may detect in certain high points the earliest signs of what will become a major advantage of Hearn's impressionism: his technique is to force the rhythm of the narration to parallel the rhythm of the events being watched. Unlike his first efforts to be artful with words, the manipulation of language to make it parallel with action cannot distract the reader from the story; in fact, it tends to enhance the reality of the scene. If we ignore the vulgar cruelty of the following passage, we will note how Hearn makes the lines conform to the increasing shrieks and desperation of the victim:

> Perhaps the thrusts of the assassin's pitchfork, wedging him still further into the fiery hell, or perhaps the first agony of burning when his bloody garments took fire, revived him to meet the death of flame. Fancy the shrieks for mercy, the mad expostulation, the frightful fight for life, the superhuman struggles for existence— a century of agony crowded into a moment—the shrieks growing feebler—the desperate struggles dying into feeble writhings.[12]

Hearn himself tended to be fanatical about punctuation, but it was not the punctuation (which earned him the nickname of "Old

Semicolon") that made his prose startlingly alive: it was the careful measuring of narrative time to a proportionate sequence of
phrases, sentences, and construction which would be marked off
by punctuation.

If we closely analyze the second climax of the story, the result is
the same. The reader is being forced to gaze upon what he comes
to realize is clumps of burnt and sodden human flesh as he reads
prose in which the phrases are set up to prolong and then acceler-
ate the sickened realization. When the passage reaches its most
vivid detail, the very phrases are glued and strung together like
the remains themselves: "Laid upon the clean white lining of the
coffin they rather resembled great shapeless lumps of half-burnt
bituminous coal than aught else at first hurried glance; and only a
closer investigation could enable a strong-stomached observer to
detect their ghastly character—masses of crumbling human
bones, strung together by half-burnt sinews, or glued one upon
another by a hideous adhesion of half-molten flesh, boiled brains
and jellied blood mingled with coal." The rhythm of the telling
has to match the nature of the object. For a travel writer, the
ability to match impressions with the words or—few enough words
to suggest how briefly the impressions were felt—will be an ines-
timable advantage.

II *On the Commercial*

The more Hearn studies ways of objectivity, the more he seems
to discover methods of heightening ordinary experience. From the
discovery that a neutral narrator can be the means of provoking
excitement in a reader, he proceeds to explore the fascination of
neutrality for its own sake. The new technique might be called
"artful materialism" in the sense that research is long since over,
reference to the researcher is superfluous, and an impersonal
orderliness is given to the arrangement of description. Several of
the early pieces for the *Commercial* are exercises in material, geo-
metrical re-examination of a single object—as in the portrait of
the firing kiln in "Porcelain Painting":[13] "The kiln is divided into
two parts, the lower portion being the receptacle for the wood,
and the upper part containing the china to be fired. The lower
part does not differ materially from an old-fashioned grate, except
that on each side there are four openings or flues, allowing the
smoke and heat to ascend and surround the receptacle which

holds the china. This receptacle is shaped like a house, the roof forming an apex. . . ." [14]

Even in the metaphor the comparison remains at the same hard, visualized level as the remainder of the passage. No report of a single experience, it is the merging of a long series of investigations; and the narrator seems to have no fixed position, no regular point of view—indeed, he scarcely exists as an entity.

Along with his tendency to describe objects suspended as it were in time, Hearn's pieces verge more and more on the fragmentary. The newspaper feature is relatively short; even within the short space of the article, he begins to allow separate, smaller impressions to group themselves apart from one another. But the whole piece still conveys a sensation of order: There is a unity, but it is that of a train, and not the unity of an organism. Handled well, each part gives off a vague mutual reflection of themes or atmospheres in which each functions more expressively than it could alone. Eventually, this approach will make it very difficult for Hearn to write a traditional novel but compensatingly easy for him to compose a reflective monologue or a study of insects in the tropics. If we observe this technique at work on a simple, rather awkward level in " 'Rags, Iron, Stoves!,' " [15] we can anticipate the more complex shifting of modes in an ambitious work like *Chita*. " 'Rags, Iron, Stoves!' " regularly shifts not only its scene but also the difficulty, the colorfulness, and the tone of its language, each time making the style underline the thing or idea being considered.

"Some Pictures of Poverty," [16] like " 'Rags, Iron, Stoves!,' " is a train of impressions. What it shows in the way of progress is its expansion of the material world to include not only human things and costumes but also the architecture of human ruin. Admittedly, Hearn is attracted to the outsiders in the contemporary world, but his is an ambivalence of attraction and superiority; he is drawn to them by feeling and distanced from them by the ability to turn them into knowledge and art. Hearn's forays into the squalor of the riverside are extraordinary in that, if he goes in order to bring back impressions of what the levee life really is, the very impressions which he recorded give one of the rare objective views of that ignored existence. Hearn's peculiar approach to artistic objectivity can also function as historic document, so close together are the genres. In his pictures of poverty, we study the bony eyes of an Indian woman, the physiology of a tenement, a superstitious Irish woman listening with insomnia to the screams of a beaten child, a cellar in which an old Negro woman is dying, and the puzzling collection of pictures on her walls. So subtle now is the re-arrangement of research that the objects and the women alike convince us of their incoherence at the same time that they are quite clearly drawn.

Best known of these studies of the Cincinnati poor are the sketches issued over a period of years in the *Commercial* and collected by O. W. Frost in a volume entitled *Children of the Levee*.[17] Together, the pieces make not just an exploration of "low-life," but a rich, varied picture of Cincinnati humanity—though we must remind ourselves that Hearn did not publish them with this end in view. In the earliest sketches, the author struggles to overcome the problems of language and research we have seen solved in connection with less unusual topics. The view of levee life still borders on the lurid, or his prose has not yet emerged from abstraction—as we see, for example, in the rape of the drunken woman in "Pariah People." [18]

In "Levee Life" [19] Hearn has at last decided on a restrained, journalistic American prose which he uses even for the transcription of songs. The places and the persons now seem to be familiar acquaintances, and this effect derives probably from the adroit manner in which the narrative passes around the tavern, picking off each personage with a vivid tag trait or reputation, and sketching in the dancers, the costumes, and the crumbling plaster with equal attention and equal detail.

In these levee sketches, Hearn faces directly the question of how to reconcile the art and the truth of the documentary. The various demands of charm—of telling enough without leaving out an important part of the truth, and of evoking understanding without appearing to be an advocate—he earnestly tries to meet. Perhaps most successful in winning sympathy by an objective consideration of the outcasts as people is "Black Varieties." [20] The presentation seems calculated to carry the reader from amused outside observer to such an acceptance of the inhabitants that their enthusiasm comes across to us as ours also. We are made, that is, to take up their point of view.

"Black Varieties" begins with an "alienated" study of the place itself—candles, improvised stage, muslin curtains. Then the observer backs around to scrutinize an audience suddenly revealed as present. He sees first what would be most noticeable: an isolated group of defensively close "depraved" or declassed white girls, and he marks them down one by one. Then, with more relaxation, his glances linger over the dress of the colored women, their men, and the breeze which they can feel. Until the extended quotation from the show, the minstrels are seen from a position parallel to the audience; but at this point, and particularly because it is funny, when the humor of the audience joins with our humor, the people in the room take on personalities and are seen from a point in the audience itself. Hence the end, seemingly a destruction of this mood of generous laughter, actually is a reasonable extension of it: it is for us, like them, the refreshment of night air after a comfortable, hot evening.

Many of the other pieces (even when they indulge in sociological learning) contain stunningly active characters. In a few short paragraphs in "A Child of the Levee," [21] Albert Jones is conjured up for us: a drunken man is dragged from the river, he is interrogated in the police station, the delight of the police upon recognizing him is presented, and his extraordinary performance of a repertoire of steamboat whistles is described. All the complex misery and career of simple man is suggested by capturing him photographically at a time when events make him be everything he can be.

In "Dolly—An Idyl of the Levee," [22] it is not Dolly's tear-jerking end, betrayed and abandoned, which matters; it is the accumulated effect on incidents from her careless life: her moonlit swims, her eccentric antisnobbery against the levee people, her yellow good-looking man, her hours reeling off her knowledge to a neighbor's tiny child. In "Banjo Jim's Story," [23] the ghostly illusions do not make us shiver; but the realistic ugliness of human pain counts: the deaths of the Negroes around Banjo Jim, from morphine-want in the workhouse, from terrified despair, or from drink like "the tall wicked-eye mulatto who drank herself to death." Hearn's very artistic distance, then, allows him to have a special skill in seeing what is really there—and in letting us see it too.

III   *"Gibbeted"*

The final demonstration of the continuity of Hearn's writing comes, appropriately, with his story of a hanging. Nearly all of the talents that we have discussed—rhythmic underlining, theme-and-variation organization, the abnegating and impressionistic narrator, and the documentary which uses the flavor of truth to gain sympathy—are used in "Gibbeted" [24] for which Hearn uses a bleak, American language. The impression of cold thoroughness is important—the brisk pulse-taking as the young victim expires and the scientific consultations of the watch—because in actuality the story is ingeniously re-arranged and focused for partisan effect.

The opening performs two duties: it assures us that the execution is now an accomplished fact and that the murder was quite without provocation. But it also establishes something distasteful: the public thirst for the hanging. Then it goes quickly but thoroughly through the respectable career and pointless death of the murdered man—a man whose mistake was to arouse the anger of a drunken youth.

On the second page, doubt as to the identity of the assailant is quoted from the trial record, even though, as we eventually discover, that doubt should no longer exist. Immediately, we are told that a hung jury had necessitated two trials—further doubt. When, in the next section, the young prisoner is described, his viciousness (of mouth and eyes) is readily granted; but this time the concentrating is on the public's refusal of sympathy and on its hatred of his denials of the crime. The blameless victim of a boy's unfeeling wrath has now been shunted aside to make way for the wrathful boy, the victim in turn of an unfeeling public rage.

Just as we are about to move from the boys' gang leadership to his homelife, the narrator breaks off the flashback to confide that his strict, realistic limits allow no room for the perhaps appropriate moralizing upon the abuse of "early admonitions," and that from this modest perspective, "the facts in the case . . . were simply that a poor, ignorant, passionate boy, with a fair, coarse face, had in the heat of drunken anger taken away the life of a fellow-being, and paid the penalty of his brief crime, by a hundred days of mental torture, and a hideous death." This set of selected facts is, surely what we have been moving towards: but *the* facts? A "poor" "boy," a "fair" face, a "fellow-being," a "brief" crime, a mental "torture," a "hideous" death? All are true, but how well chosen!

As if to rebut such questions, in the next section, Hearn evidently at a loss to find the torture of a sensitive being in the real case at hand, conjures up the frightful victim of the shrinking cell from Poe's old tale of terror as a correlative to the "torture to which condemned criminals are periodically subjected in our prisons." After these legendary and gloomy visions (the "black scaffold," the "sable hood," the "night-black darkness"), the situation is once more restated: "The victim [note the complete shift from *murderer* to *victim*] was young and strong, a warm-blooded, passionate boy, with just that coarse animal vitality which makes men cling most strongly to life, as a thing to be enjoyed in the mere fact of possession—the mere ability to hear, see, feel."

The stage is now prepared for the entrance of the transformed hero, who is allowed "one story" only, and that is reported through a deputy. This story is one of unexplained cries in the night that are heard alike by boy and deputy; to the others, the boy had pretended he did not know what the cry was, but to the deputy he had confessed that he knew—it was his mother, crying for him. Sentiment? But does a deputy become sentimental?— Hearn wants us to ask.

Then we have the appearance of Father Murphy, the repentance, the promise to confess. Only as we are told of the confession are we made aware of the boy's thoughts of suicide—which he has, of course, overcome. He has, after all, some feelings—but not too much of them. When we hear his shouts of defiance as he ascends the gallows, we are able to understand them as bravado, and we see then that they are not arrogant, but pitiful.

We have known all along that this hanging failed the first time; therefore the lengthy examinations of the rope and the trap door have a lugubrious relevance, though noteworthy for their conscientious attention to measurement and calculation. As a means for providing some equivalent of the suspense felt by the boy, Hearn seizes the device of a suspended survey of the colorless occupants of the deathroom: "Sisters of Charity, in dark robes; solemn-faced priests, with snowy Roman collars; Sheriffs and Deputy Sheriffs of austere countenance, which appeared momentarily to become yet more severe; policemen in full dress whispering in knots along the white corridor, a score of newspaper correspondents and reporters scattered through the crowd, writing and questioning and occasionally stealing peeps at the prisoner through the open door; calm-visaged physicians consulting together over open watches. . . ." [25]

From this catalogue we switch back in time to the final, pious, simple moments of the boy. Then at last he comes forward, to deliver his confession—a document which is quoted, in small type, in full. Its regret, its release of the accomplice from guilt are useful; but most effective is the impression of plain, bluff matter-of-fact contemplation of everything, trivial and enraged, that had happened on the murder night. And he suddenly appears in the hanging room, "younger and handsomer"; and the crowd, no longer the bloodthirsty avengers of the earlier sections, emits an audible hum of surprise.

The first hanging is now deliberately told in mechanical terms: documents, officials, bodily positions, operations, relative locations. But with the moment of the terrible mistake, the sentences grow first breathless, then confused with the rush of horrified deputies. Unnamed quotes arise—perhaps from the boy, perhaps the gasps of spectators. And throughout this section Hearn manages to keep hold on his main credentials: objectivity, bare truth. "In the meantime they had procured the other rope—a double thin rope with two nooses—and fastened it strongly over the cross-beam."

In the second hanging, we watch the boy; for he is now nothing but a pitiful, terrified victim of a great unasked-for cruelty. Quickly, Hearn switches from his livid face and whispered phrases with the priest to the material figure of the body, falling, jerked, crumpled. And he *holds* us to the corpse by the unusual revelation of the dead boy's slowly diminishing pulse—he is insistent on the persistence of life as it drains away, by the most minute comparisons of pulsebeat count: "Five minutes later, Dr. Crum, the jail physician, holding the right wrist, announced it at eighty-four. In ten minutes from the moment of the drop it sunk to sixty. In sixteen minutes the heart only fluttered, and the pulse became imperceptible. In seventeen minutes Dr. Crum, after a stethoscopic examination, made the official announcement of death." [26] The final paragraph begins with a quiet tribute to the calm and undisfigured body: a still, male beauty. But Hearn, determined to leave us with a sense of scientific accuracy, closes the piece with a flourish of understatement: "A medical examination showed the neck to have been broken."

In "Gibbeted" Hearn uses those new instruments now at his hand: the re-arrangement of history for effect, the rhythm of speech to amplify the motion of life, the filtering of experience through the careful selection of language, and the exploitation of human emotion by the use of narrative restraint and cool, material objectivity. His later work would often be greater, but the Cincinnati apprenticeship is apparently crucial to that greatness.

CHAPTER *2*

France

TRANSLATION is a reporting of things seen. As a translator, Hearn sketched in English the things he had seen in French. A traveler in an exotic world, he reported his experiences when he found them remarkable. Insofar as he was a mere journalist, he was obliged to be honest: he had to try to give only what he had experienced—nothing more, nothing less; and he had to endeavor to convey the exact quality of that experience—as delicious or as distressing. Insofar as he was also an artist (and we have already seen the early developments of his art), he will be tempted to go on and reshape, improve, enhance, or heighten these experiences as he re-creates them in English.

Perhaps to guard against this urge, or perhaps out of a young artist's reverence, Hearn made an awesome principle of literal translation. Because he was at this point both a developing artist and an apprentice eager to put himself to the tutelage of a literary tradition and established art, he was gravely conscious of the effective power of the word, of the justly formed phrase, of the intonations of rhythm, of the distortion of time. He was not yet prepared to improve the older text; he was prepared to investigate these recognized forms of art as they existed in the given text.

What he meant by "literal translation" was, first, the discovery of these art forms in the French text, and, second, the use of an existing form (word, phrase, rhythm, chapter, note, comma) in English which corresponded as unquestionedly as possible to the French. If no art form of that sort existed in English, then Hearn strained and combined the existing forms to create one.

Because of this determined literalness, Hearn's translations continue to serve well even today as interpreters of the nineteenth-century French works he chose. And much more flattering to Hearn, he chose exceedingly well. The first duty of a reporter is news; of a translator, it is taste. Théophile Gautier, Gustave Flaubert, Emile Zola, Pierre Loti, Guy de Maupassant, Alphonse

Daudet, Charles Baudelaire, Gérard de Nerval, Villiers de l'Isle Adam: these are the great literary names for whom Hearn elected to serve as an intermediary.[1] His final literary apprenticeship was served in this sense in France, with the generations of the Romantics, the Realists, and the Decadents.[2]

Even a literal translator, of course, must be able to decide where the effective parts of the original lie. Or, to put it in the terms we have been using, if a reporter must know what is sensational and what is not, a translator must likewise know what sensation or sentiment lies at the heart of the experience which has been told to him. Otherwise, he will be at a loss to understand the focus of the artistic devices operating in the original. He cannot be so honest in conveying all the artistry of the French that he obscures the reason for having called upon that artistry to begin with—the effect.

Hearn's knowledge of French was so good that occasionally it was even prejudicial to his English (because the two languages are so much alike in vocabulary and grammar). A French opinion of his qualifications as a sensitive reader gives us reassurance: "Car s'il est vrai que Hearn—un coup d'oeil sur les citations françaises dans ses lettres nous en persuade—ne possédait point du français un science grammaticale très sure, s'il pouvait à bon droit se récurser quand un ami lui conseillait de tenter sa chance en cette langue, il était doué du moins d'un tact linguistique très délié, et d'une sensibilité particulièrement aiguë aux langues latines."[3]

The conflict between varying glossaries, forms, and sounds necessarily makes every translation differ from its original; and varying reactions to the same forms (and varying traditions in which the forms are to be considered) distort its effects probably even more so. But every translator has one secure principle on which to hold: the version he gives must be fair to the reputation of the original—good French deserves good English; delightful French, delightful English. And Hearn's career as a young translator of French literature developed toward a realization of this goal; he moved from an obsession with the sacredness of the word of the master to a supple regard for the text and for its vitality as a unit.

I *The Romantics*

Hearn explored the world of French literature during his last years in Cincinnati and all of his years on the American mainland. At first, his subjects were the accepted masters of Romanticism; but later on he was among the first of English writers to recognize and re-present the contemporary French generation. Translation did not improve his English; it merely made him more self-conscious about what he was doing with his English.[4] Indeed, we might say that he reported on French literature so enthusiastically because each work he was translating drew on talents he already possessed.

The stories that Hearn translated from Théophile Gautier scarcely move; they are, instead, historical and supernatural locales wherein objects and atmospheres are inspected and transformed by an intrusive, ironical narrator. Certainly a plot exists, as well as characters; yet they too seem more suited for declamation or for the striking of moody attitudes than for active, interested existence. Typically, we have a vain or silly young man who arouses, inexplicably, the attention of a physically or morally devastating woman, and whose tantalizing misfortunes are followed with utter disregard for his point of view. Even the narrator contradicts himself or the tone of his story at whim. But, of course, these characteristics really do not matter: what does count are the set-pieces for which all else serves as background variations. These set-pieces may be combinations of effulgent eroticism and sighing despair or of antiquarian bric-a-brac and modern sarcasm; but they generally are done with overwhelming care for the elegance of word and of language. The effective, beautified world is far more obtrusive than the neurotic beings who gesture emptily in a corner of the scene. The sense of locale verges, therefore, on a warehouse of the unusual.

To achieve what Hearn calls the "ornate luxuriance" of "One of Cleopatra's Nights," [5] a mere attempt to keep up with the imagery of the illumination scene, for example, would not be sufficient. The English words, to have similar glitter, may require added detail; the varied meter of the parallel phrases may require a new type of joint or proportion in English; successions of plurals may have to be set up to repair the loss of subtle chains of definite articles:

Cléopâtre le fit asseoir à côté d'elle sur un trône côtoyé de griffons
d'or et frappa ses petites mains l'une contre l'autre. Tout à coup
des lignes de feux, des cordons scintillants, dessinèrent toutes les
saillies de l'architecture; les yeux du sphinx lancèrent des éclairs
phosphoriques, une haleine enflammée sortit du mufle des idoles;
les éléphants, au lieu d'eau parfumée, soufflèrent une colonne
rougeâtre; des bras de bronze jaillirent des murailles avec des
torches au poing: dans le coeur sculpté des lotus s'épanouirent des
aigrettes éclatantes.[6]

Cleopatra seated him beside her upon a throne with golden
griffins on either side, and clapped her little hands together. In-
stantly lines of fire, bands of sparkling light, outlined all the pro-
jections of the architecture: the eyes of the sphinxes flamed with
phosphoric lightnings;—the bull-headed idols breathed flame;—
the elephants, in lieu of perfumed water, spouted aloft bright
columns of crimson fire;—arms of bronze, each bearing a torch,
started from the walls; and blazing aigrettes bloomed in the
sculptured hearts of the lotos flowers. (60)

In Hearn's translation we find a toning down of the suggestive
and sensual phrasing of Cleopatra in her bath. For example,
"l'onde frissonante lui faisait une ceinture et des bracelets d'ar-
gent, et roulait en perles sur sa poitrine et ses épaules comme un
collier défait" has none of the concentrated materiality of "silver
belt" and "silver bracelet," nor the bland exactitude of "waist" or
"arms," nor the separation of the rolling pearls from direct gram-
matical contact with "her bosom" in Hearn's "the quivering flood
made a silver belt about her waist, and silver bracelets about her
arms, and rolled in pearls like a broken necklace over her bosom
and shoulders."[7] Yet, in context, the sensuality of the English is
unmistakable.

The major obstacle in "Clarimonde"[8] is the perplexing hero: a
pitiful weakling who compares his ordination to that of a helpless
bride, he abandons himself to the caresses and then to the bleed-
ings of a vampire. Counter to the evident supernatural dimension
of his tale, there must remain a continual suspicion of the real
madness of the teller, after the seed has been placed by references
to the dream-existence. Hearn constantly uses such emphasis of
punctuation and rhetoric that a suspicion is indeed thrown over
the whole recollection, especially in the scene of the bloodsucking.
The whole has the air of a cured schizophrenic's regret for his lost

illusion, however terrible. Sérapion, the unbending voice of reason, has by the end come to be the real devil.

The resurrection of Rome in "Arria Marcella" [9] is heavily burdened with pages of Classical antiquities, followed by unembarrassed transitions like "Octavian obtained only a hurried glance at all these details." Towards the end, the narrative becomes more and more whimsical (love's power not only restores Arria Marcella but also her meddling father) until lofty Octavian at last is seen from the busy, bourgeois dissatisfaction of the wife with whom he had to content himself. Hearn's flavor ranges, too, from the enraptured apostrophes to Time and Arria Marcella's bosom to the brisk list of considerations at the end.

Although Hearn fails to discover an equivalent for the rococo wit and frivolity of the Marquise's language in "Omphale," [10] he is quite adequate to the décor of the old room and its tapestry. "Être avec son mari, c'est être seule" becomes merely "to be only with one's husband is the same thing as being alone." But the description of the Hercules has all of the amused clarity of the original—"he elevated his little finger with a peculiar and special grace,— like a marquis in the act of taking a pinch of snuff" (207, 215).

A great deal of the equivocal anachronism of the opening pages of "King Candaules" [11] (in which the political life of the Medes and Persians is viewed with modern cynicism) is quite as humorous in the translation. And, when the narrator suddenly takes his tongue out of his cheek, Hearn's narrative quickly turns solemn. The description of the queen's beauty is easily as repulsively catalogued in Hearn as it is in the interminable original. The pedantic interruptions of the first striptease are as straight-faced in Hearn as in the original; Gyges' lurid passion is just as gaudy: "His brain burned; his cheeks flamed as with the fires of fever; his breath came hotly panting through his lips:—he flung himself down upon the meadow-sod humid with the tears of night. . . ." Nyssia's inverted rage becomes, in all its extravagant pretension, as revealingly psychopathic as ever. Only the final disrobing, with its sinister imagery of red ghouls and dim shadows, goes in Hearn's translation considerably beyond Gautier in its effort to set off the ultimate white nakedness of Nyssia's body as the vision of "Death herself."

With Gustave Flaubert, as with Gautier, Hearn was scrupulously literal; in fact, he acquired the Frenchman's habit of patient, painstaking examination and re-examination of each word, each clause.[12] The translation of *The Temptation of Saint Anthony*[13] demonstrates perhaps best of all how literalism simply asks of the translator what he knows about the techniques of art. In Hearn, there is an extraordinary gulf between the descriptions and the speeches; though this difference exists in the original, the way in which Hearn goes about providing for the distinction is so greatly to the advantage of the descriptions (or "stage directions")—where his understanding of the art involved is strong— and to the detriment of the speeches that the former are by far more vivid and memorable. Hearn had become very sensitive to the way in which the rhythm of phrasing can reflect and heighten the actual rhythm of described events; he had developed an awareness of the ways by which contexts and serial orders direct the reader's reception of the data of experience toward special responses.

In the following passage, the translation does not follow either the image order or the phrasing of Flaubert's version; yet it does re-create it with an equivalent attentiveness to the hypnotic rhythms of different sizes of phrase and to the immediate contexts of the various images:

> Le ciel est rouge, la terre complètement noire. Sous les rafales du vent des traînées de sable se lèvent comme de grands linceuls, puis retombent. Dans une éclaircie, tout à coup, passent des oiseaux formant un bataillon triangulaire, pareil à un morceau de métal, et dont les bords seuls frémissent.[14]

> The sky is red; the earth completely black. Long drifts of sand follow the course of the gusts of wind, rising like great shrouds and falling again. Suddenly against a bright space in the sky a flock of birds pass, forming a triangular battalion, gleaming like one sheet of metal, of which the edges alone seem to quiver. (19–20)

Though the sands precede the wind, the long line has an abstracted center; and the sharp fall at the end completes a steeper rising into a shroud (possible when the image is juxtaposed to the "gusts of wind"). The "suddenly," rather than a startling interruption to the third sentence, follows instead the pause in the punctuation. The images in this sentence are all larger, looser, just as "éclaircie," "des oiseaux," and "morceau de métal" reinforce one another's fragmentary qualities. In both cases, the image of the edge's quivering waits for the very edge of the paragraph.

Similar comments could be offered on the extended gaze and lengthened sentence, the variegated listings and the reverberating sameness, or other qualities re-created in the following: "Candles so lofty that they are half lost in the darkness, stretch away in huge files beyond the lines of banquet-tables, which seem to extend to the horizon, where through a luminous haze loom superpositions of stairways, suites of arcades, colossi, towers, and beyond all a vague border of palace walls, above which rise the crests of cedars, making yet blacker masses of blackness against the darkness" (54).

But the equally significant rhythm of the speeches does not evoke a response so thorough. Hearn chooses to draw upon the pseudosolemn conventions of Victorian English—the clumsy invocation of Shakespeare and of the Bible through "thee" and "thou," pompous vocabulary, archaic flavors. Partly, Hearn's style is due to an insistence on cognates, creating an English far more abstract than the French, even shifting the sense by strained diction. "Mais la luxure, dans ses fureurs, a le désintéressement de la pénitence" [15] becomes bloated into "but luxury, in its greatest fury, has all the disinterestedness of penitence."

In the rhetoric of the vast panoply of mythological beings, Hearn does indeed follow the pattern of beautiful sentences, each a separate unit, which is set by Flaubert; occasionally, the biblical tone extends to the timing ("How sweet the odour of the palm trees, the trembling of leaves, the transparency of springs!"); but, more frequently, the translator is unable to achieve the rhythms of an archaic tongue, or, in doing so, loses control of the imagery of the passage. For example, "J'avais les miens, le peuple des étoiles; et je contemplais au-dessous de mon trône tous les astres échelonnés." [16] becomes "I also had mine own, the people of the stars; and from the height of my throne I contemplated the marshalling of the astral hosts" (184–85). Hearn comprehends the notion of well-ordered language; what he finds difficult is the use of that ordering itself to express not only a poetry of images, but something about the speaker *himself*.

II *The Realists*

When Hearn's time for consideration was cut to the bone, as it was during the three weeks given him to produce a translation of Anatole France's *The Crime of Sylvestre Bonnard*, only then does basic word-for-word literalness come through as a principle. On the contrary, we see in his versions of Maupassant, Daudet, and François Coppée that were produced during the middle New Orleans years an attentive stylist lending himself to the widely varied individual tones of his masters (in fact, the greater relaxation and versatility may have stemmed from his having been their contemporary, almost a colleague).[17]

In Maupassant's "A Parricide," [18] as in a considerable number of his stories, there is a combination of scientific curiosity expressed in narrative detachment; sensationalism expressed in deeds of brutality, desperation, or lust; and sentiment expressed in an alert presentation and placing of information. This threefold character of the short stories we have already seen Hearn use in the death-chamber piece, "Gibbeted." Hearn reproduces, perhaps even surpasses, the studied blandness of the original:

> On ne leur connaissait point d'ennemis, ils n'avaient pas été volés. Il semblait qu'on les eût jetés de la berge dans la rivière, après les avoir frappés, l'un après l'autre, avec une longue pointe de fer.[19]

> They were not known to have had any enemies;—the bodies had not been robbed. It appeared that they had both been stabbed with some long pointed instrument, and then flung from the bank into the river. (173)

The story carefully introduces facts against the young narrator within his own defiant speech; hence the ironic phrase "je me sentais de l'affection pour lui" comes with a doubly twisted effect in the midst of his disproportionate hatred. Hearn's version has, in its choice of words, all the levels of love, bitterness, and present coldness which that key, cruel observation requires: "I felt an affectionate regard for him."

The startling brevity which unfolds the ending of "The Dowry" helps to point up the cynical Parisians who have come more and more to dominate the story of the provincial victim: Hearn has to underline the slyness of the cousin's suggestive remark. "I say that he has swindled you out of your—your capital" pauses significantly to single out the three ideas of dowry as capital, of virginity as capital, and of the duped woman as suddenly an interesting prospect. Similarly, in "A Walk," Hearn cannot quite handle the transition to the suicide because editorial prudery prevents him from laying emphasis on the repeated propositions from street-walkers to the empty old man. The earlier passages, however, have a ridiculous solemnity wholly adequate to the trivial land-marks of Leras' dull career (especially Hearn's repetition of the word "clock").[20]

The structure of "A Madman"[21] first draws us into sympathy for the old judge (his repute, his justifiable and sensitive criticisms of the barbarities of men); then it carries us towards suspicion to a revelation of horror—and increasing horrors—and it ends with a brief breath-catching summary of the more usual or with a dis-tancing from the realities. This final effect demands a careful han-dling of the styles involved (for the "editor" and for the madman). "So he died at the age of eighty-two, an object of universal hom-age, followed to his grave by the regrets of an entire people" is official prose, complacent and yet flattering. "But as we cannot live without yielding to this natural and imperious instinct of slaughter, we find relief occasionally in wars, during which one whole nation slaughters another whole nation" is a highbrow's mixture of intellectual daring and moral indignation. "What is one being?—what is one member of one wandering tribe of the de-sert?": the poetry of unreasonable logic. "Who could ever find it out?": the childlike egoism of temptation, a simpler speech. "And I squeezed his throat; I squeezed it. I squeezed it with all my might": the language of man obsessed. "The manuscript con-tained many more pages, but no reference to any new crime": a shocking factuality, an indifference made all the more sensational by the monstrous events on which it follows.

An ending that is sentimentally inadequate to the cruelties or terrors which it concludes is a key pattern that fares well at Hearn's hands. In "Denis," the victim of one of the bloodiest mur-der scenes begs the judge to excuse him: "it is so hard to find servants nowadays."[22] After the aged father in "The Old Man" refuses to die in time for his funeral dinner, the husband's consola-tion to his tired wife is "Well, it isn't a thing you've got to do every day."[23] After the huge peasant "Saint Anthony" has fooled the Prussian officers, the case is closed briskly: "An old retired gen-darme in a neighbouring village, who kept an inn and had a pretty daughter, was arrested, and shot."[24] A sense of time run-ning on a little too long so that the reader is not to be left smugly possessed of the sensation at no cost to his vanity: this demands an eye for both pauses and paragraphing. A sense of a bitter aftertaste: this requires a subtle play with crude categories of language.

For Daudet, Hearn puts on all the frocks of whimsy, cuteness, insouciance which are demanded. We cite the conversation between the little priest and Saint Peter in "The Curé of Cucugnan":[25]

> '. . . Cucugnan. Nous y sommes. Cucugnan . . . Mon brave monsieur Martin, la page est toute blanche. Pas une âme . . . Pas plus de Cucugnanais que d'arêtes dans une dinde.
> '—Comment! Personne de Cucugnan ici? Personne? Ce n'est pas possible! Regardez mieux . . .[26]

> ' ". . . Cucugnan. Here we are. My dear Monsieur Martin, the page is all blank. Not a soul!—no more Cucugnanais here than there are fish-bones in a turkey!"
> ' "What! nobody from Cucugnan here! Nobody? Ah! it cannot be possible! Please look again." (114)

In François Coppée's "The Blessed Bread" we have the tone of a learned, melancholic snob. In "The Invitation to Sleep" Hearn gives a virtuoso exhibition: each of the three sections requires an evasive flavoring from the language of the stage of life described. There is, first of all, the nostalgia for childhood:

> Quand il n'était qu'un tout petit garçon, autrefois, chez ces braves gens de père et mère, c'était le meilleur moment de la journée.[27]

> When he was quite a little boy,—long, long ago—at home with his good father and mother, it used to be the happiest hour of the whole day, just before bed-time. (89)

The middle section expresses the extravagant, phrase piled on phrase of the romantic, enthusiastic student:

> Et depuis deux jours,—deux jours de Juin, trop chauds, à l'atmosphère de bains, trempés de courtes averses,—ils vivaient là, battant les bois du matin au soir, et, avant de se coucher, laissant la fenêtre entr'ouverte pour être réveillés par les pinsons.[28]

> And for two days, two excessively warm June days,—while the atmosphere was heavy as that of a vapor bath, but slightly cooled by occasional showers,—they lived there, wandering through the

woods from morning to evening, and always before going to bed, leaving the windows open that the nightingales might awake them. (92)

And last, there are the questions and protests of a peevish old man, brief quavering grumbles or a weary retreat behind philosophy:

. . . mêmes crosses de fusil sonnant sur les dalles de l'église, mêmes indifférents dans des fiacres causant de leurs petites affaires, même grotesque en cravate blanche débitant des sottises avec une émotion de cabotin, tandis qu'un ami complaisant l'abrite sous un parapluie.[29]

. . .—there will be the same rattling of rifle-butts upon the pavement, the same indifferent mourners joking in their hacks,—the same grotesque orator, in his white cravat uttering absurdities with theatrical emotion, while a complaisant friend holds an umbrella over him. (97)

It can hardly be questioned whether Hearn has not seen the sarcastic music of rattling "t's" and flat "a's" in this passage of disgust by a regretful man facing death.

III *Beyond Apprenticeship*

The pressures and limitations of a Sunday feature column (and perhaps the inevitable artistic temptation) pushed Hearn toward an important breakthrough in his craft. This work at the beginning was only a step beyond translation—the extract, the high point, the "memorable scene"—but it eventually led to the vocation of the years before his death: the folktale renewed, the civilized story re-experienced. What the handling of fragments from the French did for Hearn was to force him to consider how a narrative had to be reorganized in order to be retold. He had to become aware of how we sense the boundaries of an episode, of what constitutes the attainment of a satisfying end, of how one unwinds the strands making up a long tale and leaves the materials for a short one quite as intense. More often than not, when he translates from Zola or Loti, he chooses one of those brilliant portraits of theirs of a breathtakingly grim reality or a sunlit humid island noon, one of those scenes from an unjudged life which constitute the allure of their overdrawn plot lines.[30] And

there, out of context, Hearn makes us fully attentive to their poetic value, even perhaps frees them from the weight of a deaden-
ing, commonplace continuance.

In the earlier, more awkward extracts, like that from the
Daudet novel *L'Évangeliste*, even Hearn's crudely cut out portions ultimately work towards a single impression; they do make
Daudet narrate an "Autheman's Suicide." [31] The framing, too, is
gross, a stark summary of the preceding novel; but with the help
of the frame, its direction indeed, we do come to feel Autheman's
fear of his own ugliness, the frigidity of his wife, even the threat
by which he once had obtained her. Only, because it becomes in
Hearn's version peculiarly Autheman's story, the included (however stunning) scenes of her rage against blasphemy and of her
strange prayer as the train speeds by redemonstrate what we already see, or they tell more than we need to know. Consequently,
Hearn's end does not draw to a close all the motives which have
been set going.

Working with scenes from Flaubert's *Salammbô*, Hearn at first
("The Crucified Lions") allows his bounds to be set by the breaks
in the original text; then ("The Phalanx in Battle") he breaks in at
the height of conflict to overwhelm us with the learned catalogues
of Flaubert's infinitely accoutered and marshalled Carthaginians.
It soon becomes clear in this reading that this section is not a
battle at all but an enormous armory, an imaginative style show
with scattered feints at action.[32] With "The Sacrifice; Moloch the
Devourer," [33] Hearn is no longer content to scrape away the surrounding context; he cuts away also at the interior—paragraphs of
description disappear, the disillusioned high priest is eliminated,
Hamilcar's hesitation and conciliation is wiped out to leave a
single-minded drive towards the appetite of the god. Those sections which in the original provide a moment's relief, a turning
away from the spectacle, Hearn suppresses; nothing interferes
with a sustained view of the bloody, hysterical mass of worship-
pers.

Ruthlessly cut, but with an extraordinary, stark effectiveness,
"The Secret of the Scaffold" by Villiers de l'Isle Adam[34] marks the
second step in Hearn's lifelong theme of death by execution. The
morbid wit of the original has been transformed into a subtle,
biting edge on the cold description. Pages of hesitation on the part
of the condemned doctor have been thoroughly excised, and what
remains of his character is the utterly polite, intellectual gentle-

man whose motives for the agreement are to remain as uncommitted as his face.

The question—whether sensibility persists in the brain after the severance of the head—becomes the focus of the only long discussion in the tale, but the tone of it is not one of metaphysical hope; rather, the discussion is a cool and scrupulous medical debate whose very intensity contradicts its detailed scientific tone: ". . . are we to believe that the very severing of the head, the scission of the spinal column, the interruption of all organic relations between the brain and the heart, are not enough to effect total paralysis in the deepest life-centres of all sensation of pain, however vague? Impossible! Inadmissible! And you know it as well as I" (46). The modesty of the prisoner, in the face of the weird bargain (the three winks of the dying eye), lacks once again all human feeling, even while it asks gently to be allowed the possibility of a failure of courage.

Again, in keeping with the icy scientific hope, the sole emotion in the piece, Hearn purges the original, during the scenes around the guillotine, of all references to the presence of an abbé, to the kissing of the cross. The last section is entirely cleared of exclamation points, even where the experimenter is said to cry "almost wildly." We cite the two versions of the last impressions of the condemned, the one bordering on regret and then unease; the other, quite vacant of observable feeling:

> Alors, comme l'heure sonnait dont il ne devait pas entendre le dernier coup, M. de La Pommerais aperçut, en face, de l'autre côté, son étrange expérimentateur, qui, une main sur la plate-forme, le considérait! . . . Il se recueillit une seconde et ferma les yeux.[35]

> M. de la Pommerais observed on the other side his strange experimenter, who was watching him fixedly as he stood with one hand upon the platform. La Pommerais collected himself a moment and closed his eyes. (51)

The subsequent lurid description of the head of the victim in the hands of the experimenter is much like that of Villiers, with the exception of one significant word: in Hearn's version his bending down to whisper in the ear is apparently controlled, not "quickly" as in the French. This change tends to hold the suspense which has been set up during the horrifying survey of the frozen expression on the bloody face. The desperate lust for existence, hidden until now on both sides of the secret bargain, escapes into view so briefly that, had it not been for Hearn's rigid exclusion of previous feeling, it could not seem so ominously significant. The surgeon's cry for God is now set off by the absence of religion in the tale, and the attribution of a *supreme* effort to the force inside the head makes the terrified hope one which does indeed involve a hopeless humanity; and these aspects are primarily due to the interference of Hearn as re-creator. Villiers observes, "Les cils se disjoignirent, comme sous un effort interne; mais la paupière ne se releva plus." The English version has: "The eyelids parted, as under the impulse of a supreme internal effort; but the lid did not rise again." For the slow draining away of the remaining desire, Hearn's version alone makes use of a prose rhythm: "Second by second, the face became more rigid, more icy,—motionless. All was over."

Quite contrary to the spirit of the French original—and certainly to its phrasing, punctuation, and paragraphs—Hearn creates a slowly settling atmosphere, an increasing quiet, a movement towards an undescribed thoughtfulness and at last complete vacancy. What he had had to find out about technique and style, Hearn had now discovered. More self-conscious now in his own talent, he continued occasionally to translate from the French, but his work was more in the spirit of day-to-day journalism, like his choice of melodramatic, tear-jerking scenes from Octave Mirbeau's "Recollections of the Franco-Prussian War." [36] His apprenticeship was over, and his travels in French literature had brought him back once again to himself. In the interests of re-creating the hidden world within French art, he had ultimately come round to discover that translation, to be fully faithful, ended with imitation, not of the word or the spirit, but of the artist himself. And, when Hearn had finished his journey to his own time through the French generations, France had no more to give.

CHAPTER *3*

New Orleans

FROM 1877 until 1887 Lafcadio Hearn was the reporter of and to New Orleans. He moved into the literary establishment to flirt with refinement in prose. Accepted by the South, he wanted to interpret for it the world. He acquired moral earnestness, and fell in love with evolution. He wished to make himself a samurai, and Herbert Spencer was to be his master. Patrick Lafcadio yearned for the finer things, but ultimately, and luckily, he needed something better. In literature, he was to try, and fail, to siphon the grim, causal puritan view of history into his stories; and he briefly sacrificed his prose at the altar of "the very best," that of the King James Bible committee. But his art already possessed powers far more supple than either could give him.

Hearn was to be the Sunday messenger from France—the translator as reporter and apprentice whom we have just seen—and ultimately of every corner of the unknown to which he could somehow find a way. But when he ran away from New Orleans—as he had from Cincinnati and as he would from New York, Martinique, and Japan—he found that the other side of the world was only the other side of himself, and that each place only brought him closer to the unmoving center.

As if released by the exhilaration of cutting his ties with the North, Hearn's first piece from his Southern experiences, "Notes on Forrest's Funeral," is a sudden flowering of talent. A form that had lain dormant, or had been grafted into a larger structure, now emerges whole: the story whose main structural device is *recurrence*. Rather than a development through history—indeed, this form involves a negation of the idea of growth and successive stages—such a literary work uses the passage of time only for the convenience of the narrator or only to peel away layer upon layer to reveal what has always existed. The method may simply be contemplation: the object is then suspended for inspection from

all possible angles; the narrator is a controlled impressionist, seeing more and more deeply with each renewed approach.

In its more complex form, the method is characterization: the
object moves, appears under differences of light and surroundings; the narrator becomes a manipulator, seizing the object in a
series of crucial experiments, discovering more and more that
family of relationships which constitute the nature of its definition. Anything—a cathedral, a sky, a city, a man—can be treated
as an object. The definition which that object receives, however, is
never a philosophical one; the sole resemblance to philosophy is in
the clarity and economy of means. Rather, the descriptive process
makes the subject richer and *more* complicated with each additional statement. The quest is not for the essential, irreducible
man; the quest is for a man in his full individuality. Such is the
case, a man considered as an object, in Hearn's "Notes on Forrest's Funeral." [1]

A certain amount of historical arrangement could be done with
the "Notes" (which scarcely make use of the funeral itself). That
is, there are a number of incidents which identify their position
within the general's lifetime; and, for the most part, these are scattered through the piece in a chronological order. But "Notes" begins with the funeral, moves next to the decline before his final
business failure, takes up his wide unpopularity, breaks out of the
frontier Tennessee of his childhood to scrutinize the regular mur-
ders performed by his brother, and so on. After reaching the disease which would kill him, the reasonable aura of history is entirely dropped: we are back once more in his virulent old age,
then again in the war, then in episodes quite undatable. Hearn
pushes us back again and again towards the man: fearfully iras-
cible, sinewy, rough, impatient, aggressively fast, unbearable even
in his repentance. Incident after incident is forced upon us until
the man as object comes alive. Yet, most emphatically, it is the
kind of vividness for which neither explanation nor analysis is
possible. We do not understand the man; we know him.

A traveler, Hearn must write a travel piece: "Memphis to Orleans." But he doesn't yet know how to handle his thrills, how to
control his stunned impressions of a new, tropical world quickly
enough in order to observe coolly what he is observing with
breathless delight. A river trip—but there is no movement in his
prose while there is a surplus of exotic beauty—and still there is
nothing in his paragraphs save hurried catalogues and metaphoric

cliché: "A sky so softly beautiful, so purely clear in its immensity, that it made one dream of the tenderness of a woman's eyes made infinite." But what could Hearn do while his practice is still attuned to the dark corners of Cincinnati?

"Red sank the sun in a sea of fire, and bronze-hued clouds piled up against the light like fairy islands in a sea of glory, such as were seen, perhaps, by the Adelantado of the Seven Cities." And, more permanently, how much can we require of an excited man who has had one eye put out and whose remaining, bulging eye is keenly nearsighted? We never cease, in fact, to be amazed by the unforced visuality of Hearn's writing. The single awkwardness of his sight is a terrible oversensitiveness to *color;* a natural concomitant, perhaps, of nearsightedness, but one which he never ceases to try to accommodate within the close focus of his normal-vision descriptions.

Five days later he has found in "At the Gate of the Tropics" the style lacking in "Memphis to New Orleans." [2] This style is dependent upon a utilization of a technique he evolved in Cincinnati: the arrangement of a piece into musical movements, each of which provides a vague orchestrating context for the others. Appalled at the unmanageable quantities of experience with which Louisiana is confronting him, he chooses to relax into a series of thematic developments of a single place or idea. So inviting does this method become that he eventually adapted it to whole books —each part of which is a piece in itself, related only by a kind of sympathy or compatibility with the pieces around it—and each piece also divides into a series of almost sufficient movements.

Realization of this technique can only lead to an alteration in our assumptions as readers: a close reading, during which we keep carefully in mind dozens of important variables as they appear throughout the work, simply does not work because neither book nor piece is created to respond to that kind of attention. It would be idle to complain that themes from the second movement of a sonata are no longer being developed in the last movement; it would be just as idle to think that the four movements had nothing to do with one another. They belong to a single piece, but any one of them might stand alone. The analogy, in the most thoroughgoing fashion, applies to the works of Hearn (and, suggestively, to other writers). The return to the technique of continuous movements is the significance of "At the Gate of the Tropics." [3]

The opening section is one impression of great activity: crowding, thick confusion of boats, tugs, wharves, chimneys, piles of fruit, stevedores—a tightly drawn, closely filled sketch of the New Orleans waterfront. The sentences in pile on pile burst with nouns and prepositions; as the scene proceeds, verbs decrease, adding to the sense of overlapping space. Then, quite suddenly, at the end, the grammar becomes altogether different . . . a long, slowing sentence whose abstraction increases progressively. This trick accompanies a gaze out to the very end of the crescent of docks: "Look either way along the river with a strong glass!—the fringe of masts and yards appears infinitely extended; the distant spars become blended together in a darkly outlined thicket of sharply-pointed strokes and thread, cutting the blue at all angles; further and further yet, the fringe seems but a fringe of needle points and fine cobweb lines; and, at last, only the points remain visible, the lines having wholly vanished." [4] There are noteworthy sections on the old Quarter balconies, on the fragrance and glitter of the market, and on the Cotton-Press monster. Equally, there are only slightly entertaining sections. The end result, just the same, if we are reading properly, is an experience with New Orleans—in this case, one pleasant enough to encourage return.

"New Orleans in Wet Weather" [5] begins with an evocation of dampness which eventually falters and disintegrates into variability of tone and repetition; but the very first part holds onto the borderline between irritation, amazement, and good humor which later is lost. The dampness of New Orleans "descends from the clouds and arises from the soil simultaneously. . . . Bolts of steel and barriers of stone are equally unavailing, and the stone moulders, and the steel is smitten with red leprosy. The chill sweat pouring down from the walls, soaks into plank floors, and the cunning of the paper hanger is useless here. Carpets become so thoroughly wet with the invisible rain that they utter soughy, marshy sounds under the foot" (208). A similar resting on the verge of disintegration is true of the evocation of the sudden damping out of sound by a night fog, "as though the atmosphere were made feeble by some unaccountable enchantment."

The unusual thing about both of these sections, and especially the second, is Hearn's devotion to senses other than sight. For the important part of the piece is a rare venture by Hearn into the genre of verse: the section, although superficially unlike a poem in its appearance, falls so readily into a complex of meters based on a hexametered line (indeed, the reference to an "ode of hexameters" in the section must be a broad hint to the reader) that one is quickly also aware of the play of inner rhymes, alliterations, and assonances. It would be erroneous to suggest that Hearn does not employ the devices of poetry to reinforce, in unobtrusive fashion, the feel of rightness to what he has to say in prose.

But, in the paragraph beginning "If you, O reader, chance to be a child of the sea" (219–20), the sounds themselves are as important as the scene. The parallels are now ritual; the solemnity is now spelled out in the breadth of the metaphors for the sea. The most unexpected thing is that the poem never quite falls into a predictable pattern; the variation is handled as if by an experienced poet:

> . . . Twenty years may have passed since your ears last caught the thunder of that mighty ode of hexameters which the sea has always sung and will sing forever,—since your eyes sought the far line where the vaulted blue of heaven touches the level immensity of rolling waters,—since you breathed the breath of the ocean, and felt its clear ozone living in your veins like an elixir. Have you forgotten the mighty measure of that mighty song?— have you forgotten the divine saltiness of that unfettered wind? Is not the spell of the sea strong upon you still? (220)

Hearn lives out the rest of his life believing that he cannot write poetry. This poem, then, remains an early experiment which goes unused.[6]

I Creole Sketches

For the vast majority of his New Orleans output, the most noteworthy aspect is its *shortness*. As a "literary man" on the staffs of the *Item* and the *Times-Democrat,* Hearn demonstrates an extreme versatility with the familiar essay; but this quality tends increasingly towards smallness, making humor and fantasy alike take on an aspect of lightness. The average "Fantastic" is about a thousand words long; the average "Creole Sketch," about nine hundred words. Frequently, he seems to be "playing with" an idea. Hearn winks at the reader as he puts on some grotesquerie or holds a stiffly serious expression as he retells a conversation in all its unconscious absurdity.

The *Creole Sketches*[7] are intimate bits and fragments of a New

Orleans that is seen with the purposely naïve eye of a startled
outsider. "La Douane," [8] a portrait of the vast gray Custom House,
entertains with a mock-dismal description that ends on notes of
betrayal—a grief over the statueless niches waiting atop the
façade. Hearn strikes a series of rhetorical attitudes: "Ah, those
niches!—those niches! Why are they accursed with emptiness;
why made hideous with vacuity?"

The language of false oratory—comparisons to Pharaonic
Egypt, sententious indignation, ponderously immobile allegory—
appears on the surface of a melancholic, continuing discussion of
the monument as some granite tomb. The building is a solid
nightmare, a sarcophagus, a "ruin as of Egypt, vast and shadowy
and dusty." It is not called a civic scandal; rather, "rivers of gold
have been poured into it; yet it remaineth as before." It is indeed
a tomb: a breath of damp air "smites" the mourner in the face
when he approaches the doors; in its vaults are indeed the "mum-
mies of Radical Pharaohs," whose figures line the corridors. But
the choicest phrases are given in lamentation for the lost, perhaps
buried statues of the allegorical virtues, their "rigid forms have
never left the enclosure of the wooden coffins," "they sleep and
the dust thickens upon their faces." In so brief a space, the intended parody upon itself works; in anything longer, this method
might well have become as unbearable as the sources on which it
draws.

The very shortest of all the *Creole Sketches*, "Why Crabs Are
Boiled Alive" (135), only one hundred and two words, is perhaps
the most brilliant. First of all, the sketch is a game: we have Creole English, the kind of absurd dialect that is built entirely to the
specifications of another speech, in this case French. The narrator
is entirely absent; his only apparent function has been that of a
stenographer, but one who is stifling his laughter somewhere in
the background. We have to unravel; and, as we do so, our delight
at our own successful, quick decoding is doubled by social amusement at the uncouth tumble of the lines. This entertainment is
inherent; but the fragment is also created with the most careful
expressiveness—in the brief space we have someone irate, volatile,
naïve, and sly erected out of his own words. More: the threefold
organization of the paragraph sets the stage, seizes the crest of an
argument between familiars, and allows the speaker to turn an old
joke about crabs into a rebuttal which ends with the perfect insult:

And for why you not have of crab? Because one must dem boil 'live? It is all vat is of most beast to tell so. How you make for dem kill so you not dem boil? You not can cut dem de head off, for dat dey have not of head. You not can break to dem de back, for dat dey not be only all back. You not can dem bleed until dey die, for dat dey not have blood. You not can stick to dem troo de brain, for dat dey be same like you—dey not have of brain.

Like the preceding piece, "A Creole Journal" (136–37) plays the game of dialect and spelling; and the immediate peculiarity colors the eccentricity of the mores as well. The "journal" idea is a mere convenience—it accounts for the succession of firsts-of-the-month. The piece might as easily have been called a "Creole Bankbook." Perfectly predictable from beginning to end, it lives splendidly up to our accumulating, delighted expectations. Indeed, one suspects that the author has only turned the old routine of borrowing, sincerity, promises, and offended ingratitude into a new context—but this, the new *How?*, makes all the difference. One doesn't say, "Sir, I am sorry to see that you prefer my money to my friendship. You may be sure that I will not trouble you again." One says it in such a manner as to reveal a whole, new person, a new sort of offended, spurious honor: "Monsieur, I not have ever suppose dat you like more one miserable ten dollare as my friendship. I not ever more ask of you one faveur. I not like you speak me so."

Just as the dialect sketches rely on our superior confidence, from which viewpoint or stance we are amused and secure even after we are shaken by a foreign aplomb in our territory, so the sketches of quaintness in "The Creole Character" (149–50) nicely combine contempt and envy for the good and carefree life these "Creole characters" effortlessly live. There is evident sarcasm in the description of the four carpenters, "slowly, deliberately, and artistically" working, and . . . "with exquisite grace did they hammer the nails." And yet, despite all this grinning and drinking and sighing, we note with what sudden great energy and purpose they chase the mad dog; we observe that the grocery owner prefers them to two efficient Irishmen; we savor all the friends, the songs—and the whole business, though impossible for us, starts to become very attractive. One of the fundamental means by which this laziness is made to seem alluring is the way in which Hearn recounts all the men's foolish distractions. Contrary to their proverb of inaction's healthiness, the story is one fast distraction after another, emphasized by the apparently unsophisticated rattling off of "and they . . . and . . . and. . . ." The piece, in fact, fairly teems with characters and life.

Even the cooking column Hearn turns to his brand of grotesque humor. In answer to a reader who wished to know how to make tartar sauce,[9] Hearn advises using a young Tartar: "for the old ones are very tough and devoid of juice." Then, with all the helpful thoroughness of a sympathetic cooking consultant, he advises on the catching, killing, and cleaning of the Tartar, with appropriate cautions on avoiding offense to the police and on selecting the tenderest parts of the hams and thighs. His final remarks are a complete parody of his own alternate recipe (which is given as a substitute for those with less time): "You will probably find the Tartar sauce very palatable; and if hermetically sealed in bottles with the addition of a little Santa Cruz rum, will serve for a long time. The rest of the Tartar will not keep, and must be disposed of judiciously."

Plus ça change, plus c'est la même chose: this technique, which we already traced in "Notes on Forrest's Funeral," is urged in a new direction during the course of "Some Positive Opinions" (201–5). A compulsive talker gives away far more of himself than he knows. The face of a diabolic man is the subtle way in which we are introduced to the *woman* who dominates this story—not her face, but one in a portrait. Just as the face is transformed into hers, the scene comes into focus, and we find ourselves listening distantly to her and the narrator as they talk under a fig tree. When she begins her strident, shouting, hysterical monologue, Hearn once again uses an unlikely opposite to explain her fascination—her voice is alluring and deep like a reed instrument, containing some unexplained danger, a musical undertow. From the third paragraph to the end, she alone speaks—a real test of Hearn's repertoire of sentences and phrases. More than that, however, the fact that she goes on speaking, affirming, scoffing, and triumphing leaves us only to think that she is answering some invincible inner torment. Certainly, the distracted pauses and recapitulations of her speeches convey only a sense of pursuing, unseen inquisitors.

From the start, her imagery is strange: thousands of eyes maddened to reach out for her; flowers that please her as much as a jar of ashes or a box of sand; lovers who come to feel her arms and shoulders and smooth her down; a kitten or a lemon "to be squeezed and thrown away." The malevolence of her pleasures is soon clear: her smile on stage is real because she feels herself forcing hundreds of young fools in front of her to a pitch of un-gratification; her mockery of the presents she receives, because then she can enjoy their absurdities, "I have tormented men until they cried—yes cried: the ridiculous fools!" Then we begin to see the terror just behind this cruel satisfaction: "Only fools remain on the defensive. I am always on the aggressive . . . they would be-tray you if they only dared." "I believe in nothing but myself—and my mother, yes!"

After greater and greater boasting, more proverbs and cyni-cisms, she returns once again to her manner of tantalizing and destroying. This time, however, she puts men through their paces; she makes them realize what she has done—just as she is doing in this long passage—and causes them to give her the hatred which is "just what I want." First, she has enjoyment through them, then an existence fleeing them and cutting them down behind her, then finally punishment by making them hate her. Hence the pitiable irony of her last remark: "and this is how I rid myself of them. The Fools!" Men clearly are her sole joy, her whole pain, her very reason for existing and torturing herself. She is the fool of all fools.

Although much is made over the issue of prose-poetry, one scarcely hears of the prose song. Yet that is exactly what Hearn gives us in "Char-Coal"—the sound reproduction of a coal-seller's chants and cries.[10] The demands of variety are considerably eased since New Orleans' street cries are a mixture of English and French; moreover, spurts of directions to the horse and specific appeals to customers intersperse the developing choruses. Cer-tainly nothing in the entire piece has any intrinsic interest, except (and there especially lies the significance for us) in its quaint-ness. The humor, even, of the last lines—"charbon de Paris"?—is no more than a part of a lost, picturesque commercial world, with all its now harmless presumptions. Hearn manipulates punctu-ation, spacing, orthography, and even typefaces to produce his effects. Except perhaps for one caustic aside from some resident's window, the whole piece seems to be given over to the language of the charcoal man. Only a score is needed to make it fully musi-cal.

> Pretty coalee-oh-ee!
> Char-coal!
> Cha-ah-ah-ahr-coal!

Coaly-coaly!
Charbon! du charbon, Madame!

As if to demonstrate how much can be done with so small a subject, Hearn comes back over and over to the street-sellers' calls. The most relaxed and the most comprehensive of these folk-song collections is the "Voices of Dawn," (206–8) with its stress on the association of the sounds with prosperity and with the still-ness of early morning sunlight. To hold the attention, Hearn is continually shifting his point of view on the peddlers. First, it is their nationalities: Italians, Negroes, Frenchmen, Spaniards. Then come close-ups of some voices whose cries are exaggeratedly spelled out in the middle of the line: "Straw-BARE-eries!" or "Black-Brees!" Two men then come forward in detail, a ferocious Italian who "plunges his blazing black glance into the interior" before breaking out into a cry, the full verse of a little rhyme from the Cantelope Man. Then there are the inexplicable shouts of the morning distance, a daily riddle: "SHE got." The quavering tenor trill of the Clothespole Man, the weird transformations of "Fresh figs!" into "Ice crags!," or the little jokes which occur to one every tormented morning—all this is done as a kind of indulgent, inevi-table enjoyment, with a narrator who cannot be so hard as to complain.[11]

II Fantastics and Other Fancies

The reveries and imaginative fragments collected under the name of *Fantastics and Other Fancies* (217–386) are, to say the least, decadent. For Lafcadio Hearn, who thought the way to ex-press his new-found happiness with Louisiana was to call it "a dead face that asked for a kiss," decadence was a natural humor. Occasionally these selections are merely unsuccessful experiments; occasionally they pass over the line from decadence to sentimen-tality, as in the nauseating archness of "The Little Red Kitten." [12] But other times, when by accident or design a sketch manages to hold back from the seductions of profundity, the decadence achieves that willful denial of reality that marks the dying cen-tury's flight toward the dream and the unconscious. At these mo-ments, Hearn's "dreams of a tropical city" have all the unex-plained and fixated beauty that no amount of invocations and cosmic metaphorings could otherwise provide. The heavy burden which figuration and eternities place on such brief narratives can be observed in "The Vision of the Dead Creole" (269–73).

The leading sentence of the opening paragraph makes thoroughly consistent and satisfying decadence combine with metaphors which we must either find beyond the range of the narrator who is making his way onto the shore, or hold to be the blatherings of the dreariest kind of *poseur:* "The sea-ripples kissed the brown sands silently, as if afraid; faint breezes laden with odors of saffron and cinnamon and drowsy flowers came over the water;—the stars seemed vaster than in other nights;—the fires of the Southern Cross burned steadily without one diamond-twinkle;—I paused a moment in terror;—for it seemed I could hear the night breathe—in long, weird sighs."

One is distracted by the problem of those silent, fearful kisses on behalf of the sea-ripples: does it have something to do with sighs of the night air—is it because the sands are brown that the ripples are afraid? One worries over the phrase "diamond-twinkle": do we have a resentful reference to the bejeweled décor of some rococo faith—why should there be diamonds in a fire, especially twinkling ones? And why should his terror appear before he acknowledges that the night seems to be breathing?

Nothing, of course, is wrong with fiery stars or sighing nights. The difficulty lies in trying to reconcile the feeling of the narrator's terror with a simultaneous feeling that the author is blandly handicrafting the sentences before our eyes. Moreover, none of these possibilities lasts for long—we begin to perceive a deeper explanation for these distracting paradoxes, and then the story turns and leaves us with an expectation that goes nowhere. We have, for instance, the odd but incredible image of blood from his torn hands "dripping with a thick, dead sound, as of molten lead, upon the leaves" at his feet. Such a metaphysical conceit does not belong to a world where flowers open their hearts to the moon. The same world, presumably, cannot accommodate the woman who had smiled "when I flung myself like a worm before her to kiss her feet, and vainly shrieked to her to trample upon me, to spit upon me!" and her corpse, which murmurs sweetly, "I knew thou wouldst come back to me—howsoever long thou mightst wander under other skies and over other seas."

Although "All in White" uses the garrulous I-narrator device, it (217–19) has one who is more direct, less "refined." "No," he starts, "I did not stay long in Havana." The body of the story is

taken up with events so isolated and so insistently sketched that
their conjunction maddeningly suggests some undetectable relevance: a narrow, walled street; an iron window behind which one
can see the reclining body of a girl in white; the passing battalion
of Spanish soldiers which presses him against the wall. Instead of
these events for a plot, the story devotes itself to a frightened
clarification of details: "candles were burning at her head and
feet; and in the stillness of the hot air their yellow flames did not
even tremble." But there is not so much clarification of details as
to convey a sense of disinterest in the moment. There is some
connection between the iron bars, the dead woman in the silent
chamber, the swarthy thousand faces; and even the narrator suggests it: "and every eye looked at me as if I had been detected in
some awful crime." But he, like us, has to be content with only
raising questions.

The story, a nightmare, has the meaningfulness of one; with or
without dream analysis, it characterizes the dreamer. The "Ameri-
cano" does not survive to offer us his free associations; still, insofar
as we can respond to these vivid symbols, the effects of association
are left to us. Such a presentation of Lust and Death together is
the main theme of the *Fantastics* (Hearn would say, Love and
Death). In "All in White," the steady hand constructing the dream
sequence does not extend to the temporarily aimless opening sentences nor to the redundant summary at the end. Since the story is
extremely short, neither characteristic has any bad effect.

"The Ghostly Kiss" (249–52) lacks the courage of its insane
convictions. Just before the end, the monstrous hallucination dis-
perses, and what the narrator had seen as a vast auditorium is
revealed, rather disappointingly, as a mere hazy graveyard. Kissing a corpse is all very well, even in the context of all these other
corpse-kisses in surrounding tales; but in *this* tale everything has
been focussed on the horror of the public kiss—for the narrator's
perspiring, trembling body in the midst of the unreasonably
large audience, his heart beating so loud he is aware that it
drowns out the sounds of the actors, provides the essential terror
of the story. To suddenly deprive it of the source of this paranoid
embarrassment is to rid the tale of all its terror: to be alone with a
corpse comes as a sort of mock-relief. Almost anything else which
would hold onto the scene—feeling her mouth give way beneath
his, a deafening volume of noise or silence, finding himself unable
to breathe or to pull his mouth from her kiss—might be better, so

long as it offered a different kind of final twist to his uncontrollable urge to accept the doom she represents.

Some of the imagery is quite adequate to the ambiguous tone of graveyard within apparent theater: "crests of palms casting moving shadows like gigantic spiders" through "far distant oriel windows" and her lips "humid, as with the kisses of the last lover." The narrator's extravagant euphemisms on the charms of the woman seated before him are reasonable because he does show himself to be at once a babbler and a repressed, terrorized rapist. Hence his fascination with the curls against the soft movements of her neck becomes his appropriated and perverted sensuality. Whatever the ineptness of the ending, the climax of his overpowering, public lust is undeniable:

> I pressed my lips passionately to hers; I felt a thrill of inexpressible delight and triumph; I felt the warm soft lips curl back to meet mine, and give me back my kiss!
> And a great fear suddenly came upon me. And all the multitude of white-clad men and women arose in silence; and ten thousand thousand eyes looked upon me.

All through the piece his clichéd ravings are distorted by perverse changes: in a passionate kiss, do "warm soft lips curl back" without some sinister resolve?

A space of four years separates the two versions of "A Dead Love" (the second being called "L'Amour Apres La Mort" [291–93 and 371–73, respectively]); and we could hardly find a better demonstration of the way in which literary status symbols damage Hearn's natural creative impulse. In the earlier story, told cleverly from the point of view of a corpse lying in the grave, there is a lightness to the narration which admits a flavor of poignancy into the brief telling. Set off by glimpses of a mosaic-like outside world (through a "fissure in the wall of the tomb"), the dead man cannot rest; and, in his restlessness, he becomes more and more weary. Thus the emblematic shooting forth of a flower from his heart towards the woman who stops beside the tomb is a probable part of this only half-real world. And the way in which even this last quaint gesture goes uncredited makes the ending as comic-pathetic as the whole, sketchily related story has been. Its delightful, to us, Freudian obviousness only helps to fit it into the playful sadness of the love-death theme:

And he knew the whisper of her robes; and from the heart of the
dead man a flower sprang and passed through the fissure in the
wall of the tomb and blossomed before her and breathed out its
soul in passionate sweetness.

But she, knowing it not, passed by; and the sound of her foot-
steps died away forever!

So the last note, quickly told, blends in once again the tiring sadness of being dead.

In the later verson of this tale Hearn performs a number of
"uplifting" surgeries. The typography, like the punctuation, the
grammar, and the language, is made fancier. The rhythm is more
stressed, presumably for its own sake. The scenery also is elaborated. The length is, for one reason or another, increased. Hope-
fulness, and more philosophy, have been introduced.

In the first version, the dead man looked "and saw the summer
sky blazing like amethyst"; the second relates that he looked "and
beheld the amethystine blaze of the summer sky." Where the first
says, "So that the dead wished to live again; seeing that there was
no rest in the tomb," the second reports, ". . . So that the dead
man dreamed of life and strength and joy, and the litheness of
limbs to be loved: also of that which had been, and of that which
might have been, and of that which now could never be. And he
longed at last to live again—seeing that there was no rest in the
tomb."

Years now came and went "with lentor inexpressible" and
when the beloved comes to stand beside his tomb (Biblically,
"even unto the ancient place of sepulture"), no magical erotic
plant blossoms; one merely blushes: "And he knew the whisper of
her raiment—knew the sweetness of her presence—and the pallid hearts of the blossoms of a plant whose blind roots had found
food within the crevice of the tomb, changed and flushed, and
flamed incarnadine. . . ." The flower blushes, presumably, at the
memory of what it did in the last story.

The weariness of the dead man is reversed and dissipated by his
reconciliation in the tomb—now he *likes* the scenery (no longer a
heartbreaking contrast) that is "not so hateful as before." He becomes not the corpse of the little man who couldn't fully die, but a
kind of bedridden connoisseur from whom the scenery is a lavish
display. When "She" walks away forever, we can't think that the
old boy will really mind.

In the opening section of "The One Pill-Box" (341–46), Hearn calls upon images from many of his other sketches of New Orleans to create a plague scene: an awesome, metallic furnace-heat that blisters the wood and iron of the dusty city. Nothing in the rest of its narrative, carefully (and capably) restricted to the stream-of-consciousness of a dying, plague-stricken mill-master, quite achieves the level of the beginning. But in it Hearn's catalogue-mania becomes realistic, obsessional impressions in the mind of a delirious patient. Even the images chosen are appropriate to the experience of a mill-man. The paragraphs are used to suggest both stages of the disease and the jumbled, fragmentary mood of a conscious moment.

The logic of the impressions is dream logic at various levels of rationality. Sometimes consciousness veers into full distress: "And there was so much to be arranged first: there were estimates and plans and contracts; and nobody else could make them out; and everything would be left in such confusion! And perhaps he might not even be able to think in a little while; all the knowledge he had stored up would be lost; nobody could think much or say much after having been buried." Sometimes consciousness falls, however, toward the contemplation of hallucinations and anxieties: "Then it seemed to him that each little box received its deposit of memories, and became light as flame, buoyant as a bubble;—rising in the air to float halfway between floor and ceiling."

The style of "One Pill-Box" is clean until the end; and there, in the vivid awareness of death, the sudden emergence of gross metaphors—"the fathomless purple of the night, and the milky blossoms of the stars"—corresponds to a mute, momentary terror felt for the first time by this man of contracts. But this is not, in fact, the last image or impression: from the heavily colored visual oppression, the narrative turns once again to the thinking man within—this time to a sentence whose bitter objectivity conveys far better than any thrill or moral the disappointment of dying.

Others of the *Fancies* concentrate upon the love aspect of the theme rather than on that of death. "The Idyl of a French Snuff-Box" (309–11) utilizes a realistic outer framework to enclose two types of fantasy within. The outside frame is simplicity itself: an old gentleman leaves behind his snuffbox and later returns to pick it up again. The two fantasies neatly illustrate the two ways, one objective and the other plotted, in which Hearn is currently experimenting. Both present a "dream of Theocritus": the first, through

contemplation of the ivory relief scene on the snuffbox; the second, through substitution of an actual dream of Arcadia in which the carved figures are made to become characters in a story. The dream-story created is much less convincing, primarily because it is too sweetly idyllic and too coy—the dreamer is awakened just before the nymph can yield. The snake image (curled erotically around the polished thigh of the nymph in the first version) subsides (in the second version) into a bejeweled allegory; the snake glides off its "resting-place" and pursues the slowly retreating dove with its "topaz eyes."

The first version, like some antinovel of the 1950's, calculates its verbs so closely as to let description tremble on the verge of motion. The discoveries of the narrator, as his eyes pass over the parts of the scene, only just hold themselves back from actual succession in time. The opening view is summary: "a slumbering dryad; an amorous faun." The following view expands the initial impression, reinforces the illusion of life: "The dryad was sleeping like a bacchante weary of love and wine, half-lying upon her side; half upon her bosom, pillowing her charming head upon one arm." The next view starts to use the ambiguous verb, noticeable because of the slight shift in tense: "Above her crouched the faun . . . he lifted the robe . . . gazed. . . ."

This use of a series of impressions to convey a sense of time into the relationships among unmoving objects is most apparent in the consideration of the snake: "But around her polished thigh clung a loving snake, the guardian of her sleep; and the snake raised its jeweled head and fixed upon the faun its glittering topaz eyes." Then, having set up this spurious historical dimension, the narrator provokingly frustrates the suspended scene, and returns to frigid immobility: "motionless the lithe limbs of the dryad and the serpent thigh-bracelet and the unhappily amorous faun holding the drapery rigid in his outstretched hand." No sentimental poetry here, no coy doves cooing in the myrtles, only the paradox of life lurking in gracefully motionless figures.

At the beginning, we know that the narrator of "MDCCCLIII" (358–61) is a speculative man. This tale is another in the series which works upon the manner in which the style of a man's mind and his inner experience characterize him as an object removed from time. The scene is the Ivory Coast, but it is once again that muffled yellow of a plague-stricken tropical city. The sickness extends from the dying into the landscape: "the river-current was

noiseless and thick and lazy, like wax-made fluid." But not until
we are fully into the story do we realize the significance of the
stress laid upon the "iron tongue" of the hospital bell, its single
utterance announcing the extinction each time of another life, as if
it passed the fatal sentence.

The story moves off the plane of the old theme of lost love to
the larger one of an awakened dead-faith. That the man is shown
to be meditative, uneasy with death; that the man is confronted
on the bare, gleaming corridors by the apparitions of winged-
capped Sisters and not the Woman whose name he utters; that the
Sister, taking his hand, leads him onward, repeating strangely,
"You are not afraid?"—these elements lead toward the man's confrontation with a religion and a death he prefers to believe he has
put behind him. Thus the final fear is a cross between the word-
user in him and the trembling believer-and-doubter in him also.
He cannot deal with what he tries to call "a dead emotion"; he can
at best turn the image of the beckoning sister into a kind of intermediary between himself and the death he believes he no longer
fears. Yet what he has her saying betrays the man who claims this
to be a vision of complacent comfort, an unbeliever's calm: the
nun stands between him and nothingness, saying, " 'Come! You are
not afraid?' "

Another personage who talks himself into reality is portrayed in
"A Mephistophelian," [13] in which skeptical outrage is neither humorous nor expository, only subtly cynical, as slowly this portrait
of a didactic unbeliever is unveiled. The tone of the responses—
the piece is structured into dialogue form—is consistently self-
confident and urbane. Indeed, it is almost as if the answers had
been rehearsed long ago; the questions have become so familiar
through either boredom of repetition or long, defensive anticipation that every attack or amazement ceases to be upsetting. Love,
honor, pleasure come up again and again; and, as the smoothly
ready replies dispose of the problems, the very life being described somehow comes to seem less fully experienced. It is not
that the refutations seem so unfair or sophistic, but that, as the
conversation proceeds, the Mephistophelian seems to content
himself with less and less of vividness, liveliness. The more he
finds human habit to be "mere . . . ," the less emotional quality
his own left-over existence can lay claim to.

For this reason the concluding lines seem to point logically towards suicide: and it is on suicide that the piece does indeed come

to an end. The tone has not altered; suicide is spoken of with the same sophisticated indifference—but his life appears already so close to complete unimportance that a boredom without scruples would be an almost imperceptible change, a slight movement toward the momentary whim of weariness that chooses death. The language has never been supercilious, or suave enough to make us suspect a compensation; we get only a sense of regretful waste, a regret which is amply met by the sad overtones of this conclusion:

> When I wish for love I purchase it, and save myself a great deal of trouble. I never incommodate myself to please others, except when I can gain a great deal by so doing; and never become sufficiently intimate with others to enable them to cause me the least inconvenience. I shall not grow old for another half century, and if ever I become weary of my life it will be an easy matter to end it without the least regret.

As in "Some Positive Opinions," Hearn utterly drains the piece of all time that is not narrative time. The entire creative attention is given to the point of view. In many ways, tone, emotionalism, self-consciousness, sex, intellectuality, this character is the opposite of the man-hating Spanish dancer; but his coolness and freedom are turned into the very means by which he slowly objectifies his whole existence, just as the dancer was allowed to create a story that returned always back upon herself.

III   Stray Leaves from Strange Literature

The last of the New Orleans *Fantastics* to be treated in this discussion also marks a pause in Hearn's original (if we may make any such crude distinction) output, in the tradition of Poe, Baudelaire, Gautier, and the larger ranges of the Gothic story. Easily discontented with these associations, however peripheral they may be in fact to the real significance of his stories, Hearn absorbs, with voracious appetite, huge volumes of materials from the literatures of the world; for he is still searching for structural materials of plot and action suited to his elaborative and emotive talents.

The first results of this extended and zealous literary exploration are collected under the modest title of *Stray Leaves from Strange Literature*.[14] We must say *results*, because these are emphatically not translations; they are as original and as perceptibly Hearnian as the *Fantastics*. If the *Fantastics* occasionally show their clear membership in some part of the Gothic genre, the *Stray Leaves* also fall by locale or persons or events into some corner of the world's traditions. Hearn borrows plots and ideas from Egyptian, Polynesian, Eskimo, Indian, Buddhist, Finnish, Muslim, and Talmudic legend; and he frequently alters, recombines, or abridges. Moreover, his sources are inevitably French or English translations or retellings (primarily French). Even then, only one group, the Finnish Kalevala tales, is claimed as faithful to the text on which he has had to rely.

Stray Leaves from Strange Literature might better have been titled *Strange Leaves from Stray Literature*. At least half of the tales concern a devastating love for a woman; most also make use of some quaint supernatural belief. Other prominent themes include nakedness, beautiful youths, and the death of a son. In other words, the stories are carefully selected to appeal to the then current taste for the mildly decadent, the prettily exotic, and the vapidly sentimental. Additional evidence for their being done more to satisfy market expectations than a true search for the foreign is given by Hearn himself in his introduction: the tales, he says, are "the most fantastically beautiful in the most exotic literature I was able to obtain."

If the tales seem more familiar than exotic, this effect is no doubt because of the touchstone of "fantastic beauty." If they seem to show a considerable lapse in Hearn's already demonstrated ability to work within the tradition of fantastic beauty, it must be because they are essentially unsuited to Hearn's peculiar talent. A merely cursory consideration of the sort of tales gathered reveals one inevitable structural pattern—almost without exception they are "well-made," plot-aligned stories. Simple tales, yet not merely episodic, their simplicity lies in the linking of simple causes to simple effects: the attention is neither to the complex of influences at any one moment nor to the multiple consequences upon the mind of any one character. The attention is given to a single chain of events, one following probably upon another (however fortuitous their entrance may be).

Such overwhelming emphasis on the time scheme—at the expense of description, character, and mood—is utterly inimical to the kind of fiction practiced and developed by Lafcadio Hearn. Although a glance at his future work shows us that these experiments in plot did help Hearn to deal with plot-form, they do not belong to the mainstream of his creative talent. He never fits himself into the puritan idea of originality in literature—that literary creativity is the forging of causal chains, the revelation of history's invincible and ironly determined paths. These stories, of course, lack the rich complexity of plotting developed by nineteenth-century Calvinistic realism, but—often parables—they not only share the earnest bourgeois concern about acts and consequences, but they eagerly cater to it. In simplicity of plot, the stories comprising *Stray Leaves,* even in the original, lack seriousness. Hearn thus appears as the retailer of ephemeral merchandise.

Although the demand was strong for new plots, they were easily acquired and more easily imported by Hearn from one language into another; and he deserves, therefore, no great praise as importer. As a purveyor of plots, Hearn was in an uncongenial business—though lucrative—to make well-constructed histories; had he kept doing so, Hearn would still have failed. Unfortunately, Hearn is, and was, largely known as the man who did what popular taste decreed; he became a "retailer of legends," a "popularizer of exotic ideas," a "specialist in folklore." Despite its lacks, *Stray Leaves from Strange Literature* found a publisher and put the name of Hearn in books; his fame was not earned by the *Creole Sketches* or by the *Fantastics.* The *Stray Leaves,* undeniably Hearnian, are so because they have all the irrelevant and eccentric marks of his personality. They do not have the good quality of his other New Orleans work—his own or his translations from the French. They cannot, being what they are. There is a basic irreconcilable opposition between Hearn's talents and the nature of the source.

One sure sign of false yearnings for acceptance exists: vain pretense of language. And *Stray Leaves* (except for the stark honesty of the Kalevala tales) is full of it. *Yea,* and *verily,* and *lo,* cries the narrator again and again, in his pompous "olde Englishe." Sentences begin with *and* or *for* or *now there was;* things do not happen, they come to pass; the kings do not speak to their wives, they speak *even unto* them. Persons are not upon intimate terms; they converse stiltedly through *thee* and *thou.* The quaint people in these stories are very much like the quaint people in the Bible, only less important. For example, this passage is ancient India: "But the poor Brahman was not dead; for his good Deva had preserved his life within the well-pit, and certain travelers passing by drew him up and gave him to eat. Thus it happened that he presently came to the same village in which the wicked Brahmani dwelt; and, fearing with an exceeding great fear, she hastened to the king, and said, 'Lo! the enemy who seeketh to kill my husband pursueth after us.'" The language does not suit the story; it does not beautify but obscure it. Those pieces which have some vitality are exactly those which generally do not have to shoulder the burden of this language, this curse of learning.

The interesting pieces from *Stray Leaves* are few in number. Chiefly, they are those in which the original tale has a minimum of significant content: "The Fountain Maiden," "The Bird Wife," "Yamaraja." Upon occasion they become noticeable through some probably fortuitous oddity, like the lesbian attraction the weary courtesan feels in "Pundari" for the Buddha in the form of a beauteous woman. As in the old *Diable amoureux* legend, however we regard it, the relationship is decidedly problematic. Pundari takes the Buddha's (the maiden's) head on her "round knees . . . kissed her comrade to sleep, and stroked the silky magnificence of [his] her hair, and fondled the ripe beauty of the golden face slumbering, and a great love for the [male? female?] stranger swelled ripening in her heart" (93).

Or, in the generally chronicled "Rabbi Yochanan ben Zachai" (184–87), a few incidents stand out because of the way Hearn has held them back long enough to emphasize their irony—moments when the mocker is confuted by the vision of the angels mining underwater, angels who turned on him their resentful eyes; when the Rabbi consumes the wicked disciple by a glance without interrupting his sermon, which goes on while the white ashes smoke at his feet. Or, in "The Legend of the Monster Misfortune" (80–85), all edification and horror vanish because the story is an improbable joke from start to finish. The notion which could have been merely bizarre—that "Misfortune" is a huge sow, and that she lives upon a bushel of *needles* a day—is instead preposterous. The distress of the king who acquired her is only amusing; the despairing attempts to kill her only add to the hilarity; and the beast's being "roasted," turning white-hot, and running amuck is just the last, delicious joke on an impossible, stupid kingdom.

Typical of the legends is "Natalika" (57–63). First of all a "moral" tale—when lovers part, virtue still mourns faithfully—the story puts this doctrine to the test. A general destroys a city; steals a girl; gives her to silly, infatuated caliph, who seeks to please

sulky girl; has the general killed; the girl laughs . . . but stabs
herself. Then enters (slightly late) the long-lost lover, who cleans
up the messy situation by wiping out the conquerors, and then re-
tires from the world. The story, as Hearn wrote it, is only slightly
longer than this skeleton; but the lingering paragraphs on the
jungle, which is just crawling with insects and snakes, and on the
broken statue of the naked maiden pouring flowers from her
clasped hands mark the work with his characteristics. Not only do
these descriptions stand separate from the story proper; they are,
disappointingly, the only sections of interest in it.

The exceptional piece in the *Stray Leaves* is the collection of
fragments from the *Kalevala*. Unusual for its crudity of style (a
merit in this instance), it is also restrained in being a translation
from the French and little more. Most of the power derives from
the repetition of incident, the striking images, and the play between narrative image and magical subject—all qualities found in
Hearn's source. Each of the three translated segments (113–38)
contains plot and a suitable suggestion of atmosphere through
mythical exaggeration. There are repeated searches for the Magical Words, the slaying of thousands of animals; repeated lies and
rebuttals to the daughters of the land of the dead; the rich, variegated gardens growing out of the sleeping earth-giant; and the
long-lasting songs of Kalewa. There is a whole skein of iron imagery: a field of needles, swords and ax-heads—"he tore them from
his path with gloves of iron"—iron nets spun by the daughters of
death with their iron fingernails, the black boat on the black river
with sands of black. Everything seems appropriate because Hearn
neither improves nor responds to the text.

IV   Some Chinese Ghosts

Stray Leaves from Strange Literature, when it fails, does so because Hearn has tried to be false to himself. He writes in a language not his own because the literary world adheres to it. He
retells stories whose bare structure he does not clothe because his
audience prefers quaint historical fact. *Some Chinese Ghosts*,[15] a
similar collection of tales of "weird beauty," is far more palatable
only because he makes two slight changes: he forswears the *lo-
and-behold-even-unto-thee* accent which had so corrupted his
style and obscured the content. And, instead of crowding long
chains of adventures in cramped quarters because of some appeal

to plot-loving readers, he discovers how to pad them with learn-ing, with guidebook information, with atmosphere, with scenery. The tales are readable; the indifference of the plots is disguised. He does not solve the problem of the *Stray Leaves;* he avoids calling it to our attention. If by chance he does expand the action, it soon turns out that he has instead suspended it—we travel in-ward for vision and rhapsody, or onward to demonstrate the ob-jective man. He is not learning how to tell a tale better; he is learn-ing how better to distract us from the tale.

The epigraph of *Some Chinese Ghosts* (from the *Chin-ku Ch'i-kuan*) suggests that the contents are tales of marvels, and that the man who wishes to see marvels must be content to travel far. In-sofar as Hearn is acting as an interpreter of the world to New Orleans—insofar, that is, as he elaborates upon the legends he has discovered—he puts into them New Orleans and himself. Of course, there are plentiful notes, even a glossary and a careful statement of sources; the dust of the archives is prominent on the borders of his pages. Of course, he introduces lovely Chinese archi-tecture and landscapes in which these tales may be authentically paraded. But, when his plotted maidens have a soul, the soul is of the deadly goddess of the *Fantastics;* when his Chinese heroes come alive to die nobly, they do it with romantic self-abasement. The superiority of *Some Chinese Ghosts* to the *Stray Leaves* con-sists of this re-entry of New Orleans—and France and Cincinnati —into his work. The Chinese ghosts are as ephemeral as the stray leaves, but they at least have been called to haunt in America.

The source for the "Legend of Tchi-Niu" (242–52) is an anec-dote:

> Tong-young, who lived under the Han dynasty, was reduced to a state of extreme poverty. Having lost his father, he sold himself in order to obtain . . . the wherewithal to bury him and to build him a tomb. The Master of Heaven took pity on him, and sent the Goddess Tchi-Niu to him to become his wife. She wove a piece of silk for him every day until she was able to buy his freedom, after which she gave him a son, and went back to heaven.[16]

With the aid of readings in similar stories to assure the authentic-ity of the supernatural, Hearn transforms this tale into a three-thousand-word story by emphasis upon the marriage and upon the *wonders* of the silks. The first section, on gross filial piety, is rationed. The explanation of the presence of the goddess is moved

to the end, making rather peripheral the lesson on the rewards of
good behavior (since it comes at her departure and not her arrival) and shifting the interest instead to her unaccountable love
throughout the body of the tale. For six pages we see one shamed,
wretched, paltry, moved, grateful, prostrated, awed Tong-yong
after another. The only significant characteristic of the wife, aside
from her profitable labors, is her "cool hand," under which Tong-
yong shivers or quietly vibrates.

The Buddhist priest of "The Tradition of the Tea-Plant" (261–
73), undergoes a temptation of St. Anthony wholly unconsidered
in the original ("he was at length so tired he fell asleep. On awak-
ing the following morning . . .") as a result of an also unmen-
tioned past seduction. Hearn added so much, in fact, that the tea-
legend at the end becomes a silly, irrelevant anticlimax. The story
is built up on a lascivious alternation of religious chants set off
against waves of temptation. All Hearn's reading was used to create texts distorted ironically into lurid stimulants by puns and
countersuggestions: the jewel in the lotus becomes the jewel in
the navel; the "chapters on wakefulness" send him into a dream of
lust whose very architecture—squirming, huge pillars, and sculptured intertwinings of naked females—is blatantly sexual. An
eddying throng forces him through the gate into a huge, incense-
hung cavern; at the height of the noise and the motion, a sudden
silence, a suspension—the monk finds himself before a single,
smooth column, "whose smooth and spherical summit was
wreathed with flowers." Then he looks beneath him, and flowers
are all about his feet, thick and soft: "An unconquerable languor
mastered his will, and he sank to rest upon the floral offerings."
Naturally, this culmination is somewhat unsuited to a legend on
"why tea is made from tea-leaves."

The artist Pu in "The Tale of the Porcelain God" (274–88)
changes from a "poor wretch" among other poor wretches who, in
worse despair than theirs, throws himself into the Emperor's kiln
and catalyzes the first batch of porcelain. In Hearn's tale, all the
beatings and the poor wretches are gone; Pu becomes a genius
and a Faustian creator whom the Emperor dares to perform the
impossible. Two things stand out in Hearn's story: the description
of the museum of the porcelains, three pages long, is extraordinarily beautiful for so difficult and subtle a subject as the varied
shapes and colors of the porcelains of China; and Pu's long contest
with the Spirit of the Furnace in which the spirit replies to each

failure of Pu to create the impossible with maddening words of inscrutable Near Eastern deities—"Canst thou give ghost unto a stone? Canst thou thrill with a Thought the entrails of the granite hills?" Here, at last, the language of King James is put to a worthy use; it contrasts bitterly with the technical prose of the moulds and firings. At last, with romantic, Promethean defiance and pride, Pu throws himself into the furnace, "his soul for the soul of the vase." This touch is un-Chinese perhaps, but how much more tolerable the elaboration makes that old and simple story of why the porcelain, when thumped, goes "Pu." The Chinese plot is mere straw between Hearn's American bricks—and only an unenlightened audience could think this tale Chinese.

The other three tales in the collection are told economically; the action is balanced between miniature characterizations and miniature settings. Two of them dwell again on the favorite subject of the willful woman, the winner over a grateful man, and the other on familiar graves and corpses. All of them, however, are so fair to their sources that the stories do little to enhance the moments, whether erotic or horrible, for which Hearn has chosen them. They remain too-familiar stories about people with unfamiliar names. Hearn, who failed utterly to acquire the disease of plots, succeeded admirably in exposing himself and in coming through with his healthy talent intact.

V Leaves from the Diary of an Impressionist

Leaves from the Diary of an Impressionist [17] is an assemblage of Hearn's later work in the vein of the *Fantastics and Other Fancies* or of the *Creole Sketches*. Actually three separate collections, the *Leaves* are based on a trip to Florida and on readings in Arabic legend, as well as on the usual New Orleans milieu. Most of them have that wearied air of the familiar: even Florida is nothing but Louisiana all over again. The travelogue "To the Fountain of Youth" (3–18) is full of Hearn's myopic colors, ruddy fog, yellow pine, red dust, purple night, and, worse, a tendency towards empty infinites—"never-varying," "shadowy infinitudes," "boundless uniformity," "steeped in the infinite bath." Worse still, chamber-of-commerce clichés erupt, sentimentality begins to seep in, and the narrator starts to doze off into *ponderings*. But all this deadly swamp of Hearn's evident literary boredom encloses one strikingly different section: the Night Traveller scenes. At the cen-

ter of this distressing hodgepodge three pages suddenly come
alive, the language rights itself, tenses. A torchlit journey through
the tall, overhanging forests in the thick, tropical darkness—a new
experience—revives the writer and his art. The unseen motion of
the boat, the succession of writhing forests in the flicker of the
torches—these comprise the new haunting which he has needed
His sentences respond to the call of the moment's breathing: suspended phrases to suggest the unbearable silences, long unwind-
ing phrases to accompany the growing chill from the dewy trees
the anguish of a bird's shriek and the shouts of the boat horn, each
echoing away in slower phrases.

In "Vultur Aura" (37–42) a starkly impressive scene is also hidden within learned local color, containing feeble attempts at
humor and history. This inner moment is a prose ode to the vulture and to the demon eye with which it contemplates man's destruction. The essential vulture is the real one, which vanishes
spiralling from the Spanish ruins. Slowly the vulture becomes the
"ghoul of the empyrean," and then a symbol of Isis, of the "eye of
deities and demons," and of the far-off, unanswering god who
contemplates, vulture-like, the extinction of nations. Job, the
Vedic prayers to Indra, the caravans of desert Muslims, the Par-
sees—one by one the religions are called to bear witness to the
vulture's patient surety of the death of creatures on the earth below. Side by side with God, "from the eternal silences of heaven—
from the heights that are echoless and never reached by human
cry—progenitors of thine have watched the faces of the conti-
nents . . . have looked down upon the migrations of races; they
have witnessed the growth and the extinction of nations; they
have read the crimson history of a hundred thousand wars."
Hearn's anguish is that of a man who searches the sky for a god
who is good and sees only the circling shadows of vultures. The
riddle, however, remains; and it is hidden away in the heart of an
impersonal afternoon outing.

The temptation toward the personal rises more openly in a related work of the same period, "Three Dreams," [18] a trilogy of obsessive Hearnian fantasies—insects, corpse-hatred, and pompous
sentimentality. The third part is unreadable. So much horror does
Hearn have of the investigation of his own motives that his reaction is generally to resort to the most egregious fads and speculations, as if aware that they could not possibly have anything to do
with him.

A large portion of his output in New Orleans and later is a response to the vulgar passion of his era for spurious profundity: volumes of pseudoscience and philosophic folly were turned out by Hearn for a grateful but happily nonthinking audience.[19] Of no literary value, of trivial historic importance (except maybe as a symptom of a sickness of the age), these works have to be mentioned on account of sheer proliferation. Responsive as this employment was to Hearn's desperate need to run away from himself, we cannot blame him for keeping it up as long as life allowed him this defense—we would be heartless to think of artistic loss.

In 1885 Hearn underwent what he believed to be a conversion; but in actuality it changed nothing. Hearn came to Herbert Spencer with four ideas—pantheism, racial mentality, inherited memory, and individual subservience; and he left Spencer with four ideas. But he now calls his concepts the Unknowable, racial psychology, organic memory, and evolutionary duty. In Japan, he encountered Buddhism and then started to use new terms for the same things: Nirvana, the national soul, karma, and bushidō. None of these concepts had anything to do with the real issues of his life—except to keep them out of sight. They were his defense against the world—a mockery of respectability by which he survived the world's jealousy and his own insecurity. He acquired the credentials of a harmless sincerity.

In the first true fantasy of "Three Dreams," the oddity is a play upon the notion of being an insect—with the memory-sensations of a man in a familiar but terribly magnified world. All the instincts and gross impressions are those of the insect; from the human mind inside the bug body come ironic, pompous human thoughts that are relevant in matter but utterly irrelevant in utility. More and more perplexed and philosophical, the insect slowly chokes on the dust which fills the wall-cavity until he finally falls helplessly to the bottom of the cavity and is stifled to death. Extremely vivid and extremely sardonic, this story comes very close to being a philosophy of human life without the interference of fashionable thought. The fetid nausea of the dust everywhere, the "labyrinths of lath and plaster," the "corridors gnawed by mandibles of timber-boring ants," all of these contribute to a vision of a dark, rotting, meaningless world—and the human knowledge that *this is microscopic vegetation* and that *this is the blind power of instinct* only emphasizes the hopeless quality of the animal urges to survive.

The second dream involves the double psychology of the dead man beholding his own corpse being washed and laid to bed for the Watchers. He cannot remember how he came to die; the speech of the unrecognizable Watchers is also riddling. Some fear which both he and the Watchers sense causes them to leave. The dead man is irresistibly attracted to watch his own face, already strangely injured; and it distorts itself as if reflected in a "hollow mirror." Curiosity drives him to believe the eyes gleam at him from between the thin eyelids. He leans down:

> Then the eyelids opened widely, horribly; and the dead Shape quickly leaped; and Myself,—my cadaveric Self,—snatched at me, clutched me,—tearing, rending, shrieking—striving to bite, to gnaw, to devour! And I, with the rage of fear, with the fury of hatred, with the frenzy of loathing,—I also wrestled to destroy . . . I struck, I smashed, I crushed,—I battered and brayed into red ruin the skull and the face, the bones and brains of . . . MYSELF!

Hearn is attempting to put into public, artistic form a terrible dream which haunted him; but the result is still too predictable, too much organized by the sentimental demands of the Gothic tradition. Since he could not objectively analyze his nightmare terror, he was able to describe it in his own terms; therefore, the Watchers are seven, robed in black; the language is calmly elaborated—"I wondered at my disfigurement only"—as if the dead *I* were more appalled at errors of diction than at the presence of his own corpse; the noisy, shrieking ending, makes us overconscious of the sound-effects man backstage. We can perceive the potential of an inner life which might be made art, but Hearn at this point had to dream the dreams of an insect to reveal himself.

VI Chita

Pulling together all the things he had learned and done in New Orleans, Lafcadio Hearn struggled for one last, great achievement —a book whose size would make it memorable, a novel. Since this book *Chita*[20] employs all that he knows in literature and art, we must, therefore, make use of the critical understanding developed by studying his previous work in order to approach it justly. More than anything else, *Chita* is a work built up on a musical model. Each of its three large sections—"The Legend of L'île Dernière,"

"Out of the Sea's Strength," "The Shadow of the Tide"—is closely organized on the pattern of musical movements. Each of the three starts in one mood of excitement, anticipation, and discovery seen through one point of view—a traveller to Grand Isle, Carmen seeking a child, and Chita beholding the sea and the dead. About halfway through, each narrative shifts in space and time to another locale, another point of perception, and a darker yet related mood—the hurricane over Last Isle, Julien and suicidal despair, and the plague. In the very last part of each (for each is subdivided into about seven parts), there is a retake of the inhuman terror of the second thematic section in which the mood and the humanity of the opening theme or section are added as a resolving counterpoint.

The passage of time—the succession of events—guarantees that the musical structure take the form of a novel; the presence of characters guarantees that the novel has foci for our establishment of relatedness as human beings to its action. It has plots, but no plot; it has characters, but no point of view. Yet every movement builds on the preceding movements, every section refers itself by contrast or irony to the preceding sections: that is, the events are organized by a tight rationale of momentary attractiveness, growing sensation, and ultimate meaning. When no one character dominates, a fiction can more easily draw attention to the context in which the people live—social, provincial, natural. This is exactly what Hearn has done—the overwhelming impression of the book is that figured by the windswept trees on Grand Isle; men seek, nature disposes and destroys, a few go on.

The opening section of "The Legend of L'Île Dernière" is well chosen, therefore, to insist on the surrounding, dominating, inescapable presence of nature—sky, wind, sea, smoke, rain, and decay. Part I, the "Legend," has only one character, the captain of the ship in the storm; and he emerges only in a flash of narrative vision as a person who shouts angrily and then disappears. The opening journey through the bayous to the islands is told in an impersonal but "you" point of view. The whole attention is on a series of sketches calling increasing notice to the gray desolation; the five trees, like figures fleeing northward from the sea, thrusting out desperate arms before them; a dead forest—skeletal, encrusted, blackened forms shading crabs and snakes—and, last, the edge of things, the sea itself and the feel of cold depths arising, the colder brush of the bodies of creatures heading in, panic:

. . . touches of the bodies of fish, innumerable fish, fleeing toward shore. The farther you advance, the more thickly you will
feel them come; and above you and around you, to right and to
left, others will leap and fall so swiftly as to daze the sight, like
intercrossing fountain-jets of fluid silver. The gulls fly lower about
you, circling . . . perhaps for an instant your feet touch in the
deep something heavy, swift, lithe, that rushes past with a swirling
shock.[158]

From what? is the question. The narrator does not answer; he
turns to the comfort that one forgets, with other bathers beside
him, this fear of the deep. And he turns to the second theme: the
great hurricane of 1856.

In this section the rhythm of the prose follows unhesitatingly
that of the storm—the first waves, the dead calm, the rising wind,
the flying clouds across the face of the sun, the bursting of the
rain, the tense watch inland as the boat shows the tempest on the
waves. Then abruptly the style ceases, and the observation-point
is sheltered inside the hotel. The language becomes documentary:
the scene is the frivolity of an elegant ball, a forgetting. And, when
the hurricane crashes in upon the dancers, the narrative breaks
forth with it and moves slowly higher and higher to take in all of
Louisiana. Hearn's descriptive power is at its height.

Only the ship survives the doom of thousands: "Long years
after, the weed-grown ribs of her graceful skeleton could still be
seen, curving up from the sand-dunes of Last Island, in valiant
witness of how well she stayed" (174). This brave wreck is the
symbolic bridge to the concluding section of the movement: the
reassertion of human life amid the debris of what had been, the
return to the island. The survivors, of course, are the Sicilians and
the Malays; and their foreign words pile up amidst the inventories
of their spoils. Relief, not restoration, is the mood: the most memorable sight is of fingers cut off for the rings on them, of earlobes
wrenched for the eardrops.

A geological discussion follows of these isles as some survival of
a primordial sea coast: thus Feliu and Carmen are introduced.
They are part of the most recent tribe of settlers; Carmen, religious, fearful, trusting, childless—her prayer book like "a greasy
pack of cards"; Feliu, strong. They too pass the hurricane night;
they too watch the ebbing tide full of wood and corpses: but the
sea that brings them a child gives life where it had taken it. Feliu,
like the captain, swims well, respects the currents; and his godlike

body in the water is what fascinates. When the mainlanders appear, they fail to make the child identify itself. The baby girl rescued from the tide remains with Carmen. The prayer to the Virgin is answered at long last; for the dead Conchita a new Conchita is given. Everything blends into the calm mood of that corner of the islands: the quiet Feliu, the sultry and bright air, the murmurs of leaves, the charm of a small girl. Shelter is the key note for this theme.

For the second theme, the key is despair—that of reviving from death in a world which has forgotten one. Or so we think while we are given over to the inner life—the only inner life in the whole novel, and therefore of the most defined person—of "pauvre Julien," who should have died in the storm. Beginning with the identification of corpses, and then stopping to rest in a contemplation of the way in which the cemeteries themselves decay, tangled in green vines, spotted with stains of mosses, the narrative moves into the suicidal bitterness of Julien. He undergoes pain, decision, speculation, regret, hatred. At the end, the cemetery itself, where he stands at his own grave, suggests death: his "thoughts darkened with the darkening, and as swiftly."

The concluding section carries Julien through recollections of his life, irrelevant in themselves and important only as they seem important to him, until the return of daylight. And, just as darkness had turned his grief into suicide, so does the morning light turn nostalgia into hope. The odd way in which the sun illuminates the haze of frost is the reason he decides to go on living. And so Chita's father, in New Orleans, survives temptation.

Only the first section of the final movement is really Chita's. She is a little girl of the city who forgets what she knows while acquainting herself more and more with the simpler, harder facts of the sea's border. There is the forbidden tomb, a ruined one where she sees a skull and its smile and no eyes; there is the sea itself, and learning to swim, learning not to fear. *Si quieres aprender a orar, entra en el mar* (If you want to learn to pray, go into the sea). Only when Feliu teaches Chita to swim does she forget her terror of the presence of the sea, one she thinks bigger than God's. And the sea heals her: "the monster, whose cool embrace at once dispelled all drowsiness, feverishness, weariness. . . ." The narrative here is always distanced from Chita and is always merging into hymns and invocations of the living spirit of her vibrant world, the eternal waters on whose face first appeared the dry

land. Chita is an emblem of innocence at the midst of a celebra-
tion of nature's bright, awesome creativity.

The next section is the plague: midsummer in burning city. The
plague is in the air, stifling, chafing the lungs; a stale smell; water
speckled with something saffron. Nature hangs over the city like
some vast punishment: "The nights began with a black heat;—
there were hours when the acrid air seemed to ferment for stagna-
tion, and to burn the bronchial tubing;—then, toward morning, it
would grow chill with venomous vapors, with morbific dews—till
the sun came up to lift the torpid moisture, and to fill the buildings with oven-glow" (235).

Suddenly we realize that eleven years have passed and that we
are back with Julien. Once again weary of life—not of his own but
of the cruel portions of the defeated old Southern families—Doctor Julien leaves to attend a patient on the Isles who will never live
to see him. He also travels across the bayous, but the visions are
not as before: he sees mainly the happy innocence of the eating
and singing Italian boatmen who ferry him across; and he groans
to himself with regret and with hatred for cities—as if they had
caused his discontent. Alone on the Isle he too sickens from the
plague, but in the very house where Chita lives. Just as he falls ill,
he beholds her with nothing but incomprehension and regret. He
then loses control of his mind. And Julien, like the city at the
beginning of the movement, is stricken down by decay and disease. The last paragraphs of the section are, like the first, delirium.

The final concluding section is the most deeply arranged counterpoint: we move back and forth from Carmen's prayer and
soothing to the maddened or sorrowing waves of Julien's dying
mind. Joining the two is the wind; rising with a storm from the
sea, it leaves Carmen dependent on her faith alone and makes
Julien hear the whisper of his dead wife calling to him. The wind
takes him, as nature has always decided things in the story; and
he feels himself losing his wife as the world turns dark and cold.
But the last notes are those of Carmen, the small human, still sur-
viving, in her prayer:

. . . all the shore shook and blanched before the calling of the sea.
    And Carmen, kneeling at the feet of the dead, cried out, alone in
the night:
    'O Jesus misericordioso!—tened compasion de él!' (257)

In *Chita,* Hearn is not interested in the causes (other than racial) of personality or behavior; people are positioned in his scenes to enact what they are. He is not interested in showing a "tight web of decision, catastrophe, and retribution"; he displays a music of human beings in a world he has imagined. And, like a piece of music, though it has a development, the novel does not prove anything. It may be about Louisiana, but it does not reproduce the state; instead, it orchestrates a series of effects. There are small plots in *Chita*—for instance, "will the boat make the pier?" or "will Chita and Julien be reunited?"—but they are so unimportant that Julien and his wife do not even appear in the scene of the last ball; moreover, Chita scarcely appears in a novel dedicated to her spirit of innocent survival. The improbabilities and oversights do not, of course, matter: they are not used to further the ulterior needs of any plot—Julien comes to Carmen's to die, an unbelievable coincidence; but nothing comes of this incident anyway except his brief, aborted conversation with Chita. Anywhere he died, Julien would have longed for his wife, have held onto the hand of a Carmen, or have seen his wife's face on the shadow of some nurse. *Chita* contains not a real historical world full of the supervision of destiny, but a succession of pieces from a world which match like a mosaic.

An enormous amount of space is devoted to things inefficient for speeding along events to some supposed unraveling and conclusion—and unfortunate is the reader who thinks himself reading to that end! There is, in fact, never too much space without *some* kind of attention-holding material, however irrelevant to the childhood of Conchita—readers have been forced to admit that. They have said, too, that *Chita* shows a great deal of unity of tone—despair, death, destruction; or, contradictorily, pantheism, teleology, sentiment, but especially *locale* (to which both characters and narrator turn so often). They have also said the novel is really about Nature.

What needed to be said was that *Chita* is a skilled structure of mutually enhancing narratives, and that these ultimately belong to one great vision of men within nature—a vision whose clarity is more important than its reason. Rhythm, sensation, color, recurrence, and, above all, the musical organization of experience—to achieve these qualities Hearn put all his powers to work in creating *Chita,* a small novel but his largest work.

CHAPTER 4

The West Indies

FROM a "Midsummer Trip to the Tropics" (1887) to a "Winter Journey to Japan" (1890), Lafcàdio Hearn's voyage into the South carried him to regions even warmer, to jungles even richer, to mulatto Creoles even stranger; yet the tropical edges of North America did not provide the answer to his midsummer quest; and his disappointed hopes ended in a winter retreat across the cold landscapes of the North. Circumscribed by the seasons, this period in Hearn's life and work, like its locale, was an exaggeration of what he had done in New Orleans. He remained the reporter, but now his restlessness became undeniable. He found Martinique, and it exhausted him within a year. He found a well-made story, *Youma;* its conception is admirable, its development is balanced, and its effect is likewise moderate. He created sincere sentiment, *Lys;* and it is so bad that even the American publishers would not accept it. Only by running away again, rejecting and rejected, was Hearn able to turn things right. The quest led nowhere: the flight led to discovery.

The two volumes of *Two Years in the French West Indies* divide into two related segments: "A Midsummer Trip to the Tropics" and "Martinique Sketches." [1] Many elements of the "Midsummer Trip" reappear in the "Sketches"—not only things (like the *porteuses,* the *fer-de-lance* serpent) from the Martinique landscape, but also certain larger themes, particularly that of the colors and allure of human flesh. Hearn reminds one of an American Baedeker writing on fauna and flora. The " 'Pa Combiné, Chè!' " at the end of the "Martinique Sketches" is both a summary and a rejection of the vision of the tropical world whose motif interpenetrates the "Midsummer Trip" as much as the "Sketches" themselves. The quest for a Bali Hai never is given in so many words—Hearn poses as the traveller, the curious man—but his "disappointments," or disapprovals, do come across openly; the early and humorous enthusiasm of the first parts of the "Midsummer Trip" slowly dissipates; and so we come to feel that a search is being made. Martinique seems, temporarily, to be the solution; but it, too, betrays him.

I "A *Midsummer Trip to the Tropics*"

"A Midsummer Trip to the Tropics" is marked into thirty-three sections of about one thousand words each, but even this description is inadequate to express its fragmentary, impressionistic quality. Frequent ellipses show pauses in the recording or in the resetting of material. Scenes I to VI form the only real narrative unit, linked by a continuing joke about "really blue" water, in which each new day brings a new and more profoundly blue blue to the traveller's incredulous view. Not only Hearn's own peculiar color mania but clichés from the sunset-and-forest school of travel literature ruin whole pages of this sketch.[2]

The one steadily interesting part is to be found in the Martinique chapters, XI to XXI, during his short stopover on the island (the "Martinique Sketches" are the fruit of the next year's stay). In this section, the hints which have erupted, on the sexuality of the Negro race, become explicit; in XII, the narrative wavers back and forth between abstracted considerations of the intermixture of bloods and a nearly lurid contemplation of the moving sheen of dark skins which range from yellows to reds to browns to blacks.

This old favorite, erotic anthropology, Hearn manages in all of its patronizing, ogling, decadent appeal. From the first page— where a young man turns on him a pair of "peculiarly luminous black eyes"—Hearn makes the expressive flesh of the Creole the main attraction of his marine fair. The story begins with the scene of the naked boys on the coasts: "little boys come down, leading horses;—they strip, leap naked on the animals' backs, and ride into the sea—yelling, screaming, splashing, in the morning light . . . a fine brown color, like old bronze." (22) Half-naked black boatmen are "great black apes" against the sunset. Naked canoe-boys, "from a fine clear yellow to a deep reddish-brown or chocolate tint," are watched as if their movements were anatomical demonstrations—"admirably rounded limbs, delicately formed extremities." Workmen walk about smiling and rippling their muscles.[3] Soon it is the turn of the black women: even prudery does not save them from delighted inspection.

The significant parts of "A Midsummer Trip" are few and brief.

A proper reading of this long string of impressions is selective: in
II, where Hearn plays the Mark Twain part of the irrepressible
innocent; in VII, where the scintillating fogs and lights of Santa
Cruz turn Hearn's blurry color-vision to sense; in XIII, where a
feast of fish and vegetables in the market leads up to a rhapsody
on the lush colored flesh of the people themselves. In both descriptions there is a curious use of the disgusting (wormy feelers,
spiny husks, heart of palm eaten by grubs), which must relate
somehow to the forbiddenness of the amply suggestive availabil-
ity of human fruit (a metaphor which Hearn uses to climax this
orgy of soft, pulpy, reverberating fleshes).

Or, in XV, the legion of monstrosities, "staggering . . . push-
ing out great knees," which he conjures out of yet another jungle;
in XXXI, the joke at the expense of a ruined British city; in XXIV,
the combination of two themes—nausea and uneasiness—to produce a suddenly realistic effect: vapors, the soundings in the shal-
lows, sickly air, a weary traveller recalling the penal colony,
sharks on a corpse, the marshy coast, odd echoes of whistles and a
shot, and last, "vessels becalmed everywhere speck the glass-level
of the sea, like insects sticking upon a mirror."

But the finest piece is Chapter XVII, where, combining nausea
and fear, the attention is given to the deadly jungle viper, the *fer-
de-lance*. With a loving care for prepared effect, Hearn carries us
from an evolutionary apocalypse through all the gaudy varieties
of the serpent species to increasing delights on the worse possibilities of the poison: "Even when life is saved the danger is not over.
Necrosis of the tissues is likely to set in: the flesh corrupts, falls
from the bone sometimes in tatters; and the colors of its putrefac-
tion simulate the hues of vegetable decay—the ghastly grays and
pinks and yellows of trunks rotting down into the dark soil. . . ."
(59–60) Then to make sure we feel all the sentiment of the Hideous, he concludes with a gloomy prospect of the "surplus of its
[the viper's] swarming."

II *"Martinique Sketches"*

"Martinique Sketches" is also subject to this inner tendency
towards breakdown; even the roman-numeral chapters we might
expect are not enough—other divisions by ellipses and breaks are
frequent. But, unlike the parts of the "Midsummer Trip," the Martinique pieces usually have such a clear, overall purpose that the

reader feels uneasy when searching for mere moments of choice impressionism. Through the "Sketches" as a whole run some unifying traits: links of one topic dominate one sketch and briefly illuminate another (like the mention of "terrible Père Labat" in the "Grande Anse" before we go on to his portrait in "Un Revenant," or the conventions of "Les Porteuses" providing a grounding for the story of "La Guiablesse"); a custom of holding over explanation of some strange term until a later sketch; the turning of essays into folktale collections, of travel sketches into romances, of biography into fiction. Above all, there is Hearn's clearly fine understanding of the local Creole dialect—demonstrated by his transcriptions and by his painstaking expositions. Nevertheless, though the collection is longer than any previous possible or real collection of his works on a single locale, the increased expenditure of effort does not appear to produce a parallel increase in material worthy of his talent. If a phantom dream of the tropics does not weaken him, a phantom dream of recognition does. There are fourteen Martinique sketches—only a few of them are important.

The first of these important ones is "Un Revenant" (176–221), a title full of irony in that its subject, Père Labat, was neither the ghost the Creole legends had made him nor the returner to his beloved Martinique that he had so long wished to be. The result is almost as if Hearn sees that he is writing neither story nor biography, but putting together a man as object—the technique of "recurrence" we have seen him already develop in his earlier work.[4] What impresses him about the sources he consults, he says, is "not so much the recital of singular incidents and facts as the revelation of the author's personality." By a carefully placed rearrangement of data from the life of Père Labat, Hearn gives a life to the process or revelation itself, suspense, reversals, disclosures —none of which happens to Père Labat, only to the reader.

Because it was Père Labat who gave to Martinique the name "Le Pays des Revenants," Hearn plays upon the double-meaning of the word *revenants,* moves through the ghost-legends around his name, building them and then dismantling them himself. The factual Père, too, undergoes a cyclic process: first he is revealed in aspects that win him good will and that make him admirable —adventurer professor, ingratiating voyage-companion, exact scientist, inventor-manager-genius. Then he is the odd but notable man in enforced retirement—soldier, producer, companion of

pirates, deluder of Spaniards. And, last, his glamor is retracted and
the aura of credit is bestowed—as writer, as unscrupulous wit, as
demure skeptic, as gourmand; as cruelly indifferent to the pain of
animals, as credulous to voodoo, and torturer of Negroes.

While remaining the same man, Père becomes richer and richer
as an individual. Everything is told for the sake of its effect *as* it
appears. Unfortunately, having achieved so much, Hearn digresses about Religion, Piety, and Superstition in Martinique; and
he caps this fault with an unbecoming gush of apostrophe to the
almost forgotten Père. We have to conclude sadly that Hearn still
did not know the value of his own art, and surrounded it with all
the falsehood of Prestige.

In "La Guiablesse" (222–44) the difficulty is similar: the talent,
for a rhythm of passion, is exercised, but in a context so over-
wrought with clichés of scene and vocabulary that we must despair of the story while we bewail the extravagance with good
technique. The emotional order is correct (we know the woman is
a *zombi*): lust, setting day, the side path, fear, fear of losing her,
the cold hand pulling the hero, the ridge path, the tempting lust
rising, horror . . . falling death. The action of climbing accentuates the increase of terror and desire. And the proportion of the
phrases keeps pace with the breathing of the man, easy, doubtful,
trembling, protesting, lusting, yielding. Only the verbiage destroys the effect again and again: Hearn combines Creole French
conversation with pompously indifferent English, an English all
out of tune with the simple man whose point of view it otherwise so adeptly represents.

In "La Pelée" (310–60), as in too many works, travel is predictable: the piece must be longer, the road then must be exhaustively
described—in the dismal manner of the Very Best travel books:
"Then you reach a plateau covered with cane, whose yellow ex-
panse is bounded on the right by a demilune of hills sharply an-
gled as crystals;—on the left it dips seaward; and before you
. . . ." These hand directions make the sketch a guidebook, not a
recreation of experience. The reader is expected to come onto the
scene and do his own rapturing by means of these pointers—far
be it from the reporter to impose any further beauty on the self-
evident charms of nature! Seven chapters of itinerary follow, or
quotes from salient government reports, or worse. Then Hearn
suddenly wakes up: no number of ridges and *mornes* have prepared him for the route just below the peak of the volcano; and so

his evident boredom and forced, dutiful interest evaporate. The sketch never ceases to be objectively informative; and the description is clear, in Hearn's old language-of-the-fact manner.

The climb must have been hard, but it does not seem so: the narrator has so much time for a very clear vision of rocks, of ferns, of masses of moving clouds. But atop the peak, the fragmentary nature of the visions, each one detailed and luminous, but succeeding one another rapidly and haphazardly, manages to convey both the awe and the excitement of the climber. Amid our sense of the weakness of the inspiration, we are inescapably aware of the regretful thrill Hearn gets at realizing how far he has indeed come: "With the diminution of the warmth provoked by the exertion of climbing, you begin to notice how cool it feels;—you could almost doubt the testimony of your latitude. Directly east is Senegambia: we are well south of Timbuctoo and the Sahara—on a line with southern India" (358). We feel these are facts he already had memorized, not observations he took down from a map. The effect they have is to say, "here I am south of India, and all I feel is that I know a great deal . . . and feel very little." Halfway through his "Martinique Sketches" we feel, high atop Pelée, that they are already over.

"Bête-ni-pié" [5] is designed to inspire *disgust*. The single-minded sensationalism behind the piece organizes all its four sections as an orchestration of effect. Part I uses the device of increasing volume to direct the presentation of a listing of insect and reptile house-annoyances in Saint Pierre. The opening is pleasant—there are no mosquitoes because the town is washed clean by the rivulets in the streets. The next segment is only mildly unpleasant—various inevitable or detestable creatures are brought forward, and a hint is given toward the main scene: one should examine one's bed and clothing. Hairy spiders, enormous roaches, terrified if silly superstitions on the lizards are mentioned; and finally the *bête-ni-pié*, the huge centipede, appears in more and more distressful attack capabilities, the poison, the length, the choleric endurance, the difficulty of killing, the strange overtones of the name itself.

Part II is a poem in prose about the centipede's power to revolt the onlooker. Enhanced by the accompaniment of speculations about the why of its repulsiveness (and the answers never convince), the real topic of the section is the unreasonable horror itself. In the following discussion, the logic works only to increase

the sense of perplexity and the feeling of something monstrous in
the very movement of the centipede:

> . . . its movement—multiple and complex, as of a chain of pur-
> suing and interdevouring lives: there is something about it that
> makes you recoil, as from a sudden corrupt swarming-out. It is
> confusing—a series of contractings and lengthenings and undula-
> tions so rapid as to allow of being only half seen: it alarms also,
> because the thing seems perpetually about to disappear, and be-
> cause you know that to lose sight of it for one moment involves
> the very unpleasant chance of finding it upon you the next—
> perhaps between skin and clothing.

Part III dramatizes what Hearn has already achieved by detail
and by mystification. He undergoes a personal battle with a *bête-
ni-pié*, nearly a foot long, greenish-yellow against the black cloth
of the coat he has flung from him—"and pink legs, and a violet
head." The combination of danger and revulsion in all the maneu-
vers, the horrified fascination Hearn has for the "undulations of
livid color" flowing over the beast's body, "the panic of his legs,"
but, worst, the power it has of dilating its shape, of magnifying or
contracting itself at will—these things keep the battle exciting.
Not only cunning, the thing is aggressive; and, until Hearn picks
up the limp, contracted carcass, neither the beast nor Hearn
ceases to be a vivid character. And the unusual thing about this
work is that Hearn is nearly able to act himself in his own story.
Always previously he has been the man with the mask—the reporter, the collector, the translator, the buffoon, the manipulator
of ghosts and vampires. Now, as the West Indies provides him
with less and less, his own rancor becomes unavoidable and he
himself figures larger in the world of his "impressions."

Part IV is relaxation, a breather to conjure away from the
reader all the loathing of the middle sections. But Hearn uses a
trick: a friend shows Hearn the dried body of a plant which re-
sembles a cluster of centipedes; then, in its place, the lovely original shape of the flower. The tone of the ending is a reassuring one,
the flower is beautiful; it, too, has a name and classification
among things.

The opening section of " 'Pa Combiné, Chè!' " (87–110) puts
together the themes of the other sketches: flesh-fruit, Creole cook-
ery, childish Creole prattle, tropical haze, little statues of the Vir-

gin, superstitions, kindnesses, gratuitous grief—a virtuoso résumé and a dismissal. Despite the avoidance of an "I" point of view, the piece is almost autobiographical, so evident is its bitterness. Part II rises to heights of self-satisfaction in gaudy prose; and then, at the climax of worship of the tropics, Hearn pauses to let us look again through the medium of a cold, disillusioned language—hints only of disaster, the facts we chose to ignore, the hopes we guarded from reality.

Part III studies the period during which tenuous illusions yet remain and flourish; and then it subtly transforms these tropical splendors into tropical miasmas. IV is the inescapable acknowledgment of defeat—the robust man continually besieged by a relentless power, from within and around him. "But this is no mere languor which now begins to oppress him;—it is a sense of vital exhaustion painful as the misery of convalescence: the least effort provokes a perspiration profuse enough to saturate clothing, and the limbs ache as from muscular overstrain;—the lightest attire feels almost unsupportable;—the idea of sleeping even under a sheet is torture, for the weight of a silken handkerchief is discomfort" (98). But most devastating are the pain of thought, the feverish coma which overtakes the mental life, the weak shrinking of sensation to the merest passage of physical impressions.

And then, in Part V, the piece grows much more personal—not because the point of view leaves the constant "you" subject, but because it treats of the irritable dread of an intellectual man away from his books—for Hearn, the reader in Martinique, is far away from libraries, from reviews, and weariest at the boredom of paradise. Hungry in a way no one around him hungers, the lonely thinker contemplates his irremediable foreignness. And in the background lies another, greater hunger, the infinite maw of Nature: "the sound of the mandibles of enormous roaches devouring the few books in your possession." But Nature has a surgery for revolt and weariness—blinding sunstroke to kill the inner man; malarial fevers to make him long for peace and warmth; and, last, its grown children, the naïve islanders, to soothe the man, like sweet, colored angels. This series of vivid pictures of the ultimate destruction makes up Part VI. It ends in a most ironic grateful joy—the vanquished slave thanking the master for being allowed to die.

Then, once more, in the last part, the narrative shifts. The former sections have seduced, beaten, enraged, and at last subdued

the stranger; but we have only yet a hint of how much this stranger is Hearn himself. In Part VII what has been generalized narrative is made drama: an incident is made to express and employ
all that has been proved before. The narrator becomes an "I"—an
observer, sentimental and horrified—who retells one scene in the
life of a stranger he chooses to call "Félicien"; and the name and
the scene alike bitterly underline the irony of paradise. We are no
longer required to experience the blinding beauty of the tropics;
instead, we are forced to behold the experience we have under-
gone in the first sections from the outside: the foreigner not as
human hero even in defeat, only as pitiable animal victim.

Félicien lies sick and dying, but the narrator does not look
much at him. What fills these last pages are the sounds and the
vibrant splendors of the large jungle world above and below
them; there is nothing the friends have to say to each other—the
visit is spent in mute contemplation of the scene in which they
exist. Hearn's evocation of a tropical evening is extraordinarily
good, but that is not their real point in the context. The descriptions here are more than lovely in themselves: the preceding context has made this contemplation the very demonstration of the
mindless dream.

Suddenly a voice comes out of the night, the voice of Félicien's
slender half-breed nurse and lover, "Pa combiné, chè!"—(don't
think like that). As she caresses him and as he protests smiling, she
repeats the phrase, adding, "if you love me, please, don't think
that way, don't think." And the narrator, the objective "I," sees her
as the "exotic . . . savage . . . supple . . . witchery . . . sensuous," as the spirit of "Nature made golden flesh and as murmuring to each lured wanderer" *do not think*. Here it all comes back,
from all the Martinique sketches: the temptation, the poison in
the fruit, the vacancy behind the bright glare and the heat, the
deadly sweetness of soft flesh and soft words—nature and natural
woman, bliss and nothingness, but nothingness and bliss.

The voyage back, "Lys" (126–41), is weary with disappointment and despair. The fiction and the style are too false for even
American readership: all that survives of the sentimental girl and
her voyage are some specimens of revolting rhapsody imagined
for her by her fellow-traveller—and Hearn is at the basest of his
linguistic pretensions. The rest, the travel, is washed-out and not
even interesting in its poverty.

Youma (261–371) is a determined, conscious impulse to turn the islands to a profit—to make a regular, realistic novel out of research and deliberation. In a hundred and ten pages, a story is neatly put together out of sociological observation, historical tradition, and French theatrics. Since the occasion is the slave-rebellion on Martinique, we must have revolution scenes in the style of Dickens or Manzoni. The heroine is an ignorant, pious, attractive slave; hence the story builds itself around the old French struggle between *love* and *honor* in which the heroine is torn by Christianity and loyalty from her skeptical, revolutionary lover. Back and forth we go, as now passion, and then duty, wins or weakens. The prose is readable, even gracefully informative. The distractions are always relevant—scene-setting, sexual symbols and dreams, historical notes, and even the inserted folktale which belongs to the innocence and indulgence of a heroine who is also a slave-nurse. Hearn achieves the well-made, plotted novel toward which the literary fads have sent him: and, *sensible, suitable,* it possesses all the respectable virtues, but is *dull.*

III   Karma

If sanity is disastrous for the Hearn of this period, the unregenerate madness of his next novel is so incredible as to be triumphant. Stunned by its continual ravings, the reader of *Karma*[6] is obliged to grant that the lushest, most awful prose, put in the hands of a madman, is a sensational battering-ram on attention. All depends in the novel upon point of view—the piece gives itself over almost entirely to the world as it is experienced by a self-torturing coward. We see existence through his terrified, intellectual dread; for that reason *Karma* can only be called a sentimental horror story. From beginning to end of this brief (and thereby safely intense) fiction, we are awash in a sea of paranoid self-expression, the weepy yearnings of a hopeless romantic:

. . . human flowers that bloom only in the higher zones of aspirational being,—even at the verge of God's snow-line. . . .

. . . viewlessly your being has become slowly interorbed with hers;—each life is secretly seeking union with the other through weaving of wishes unconfessed. . . .

. . . her blood has learned of you in the blind sweet pink chambers of her life. . . .[7]

Nearly all of these amazing specimens of linguistic decadence are spewed out in the context of still more lurid gush.

What sustains us in our confidence about the narrator's derangement is the contrast between his demented monologues and the utterly hard, unimaginative comments of the woman by whom he lacerates himself under the name of love. The sustained frenzy of the passages portraying his mental existence is interrupted crudely by the bland, indifferent statements of the woman before whom he is grovelling in the dialogues. He is all blushes, quivers, hesitations, aspirations; her sole range of feeling is from slight annoyance to steely contempt. Between pages of his doubts and indecisions, she meets with him, humiliates him, says little more than "write me a short history of your life." When he finally is able to write and also to confess having had another woman, she turns from rigid formality to crushing superiority: again and again she is described as "steel," "knife," "lens of ice," "terrible," "thunderbolt," as the unforgiving masculine tyrant-woman.

"Suffer, suffer" is her message; the more he dreads and hates her, the stronger is his physical desire; and with that livid desire comes one to be wounded, devastated by her. The novel is organized in segments to apply with full force the sensation of an orgasm of pain. She makes him humble himself absolutely, relinquish all his dignity, before she will consider him—and then, after his soul is bled dry of shame, she gives him the slash, refuses to forgive him, sends him away.

There is, in *Karma,* only a minimum of development—as far as event is concerned—but there is a thorough fullness of situation. *Karma* may be either Hearn's revelation of the madman within himself or the daring creation of a perverse sentimentalist. In either case, the work is a unified raving set off against the vicious excitements of an unnamed She, a tribute to the artistry of pain. By enforcing upon realism a greater vividness—that of masochism and consistent excitability—Hearn at long last achieved his goal of a created world and style which would be stranger than the actual ones.

IV   *"A Winter Journey to Japan"*

Karma grew out of the emptiness left by the failure of the quest in the Indies; the journey to the South had ended, the re-creation of the Creole tropics had ceased. Opposite the failure of the "Midsummer Trip" to the island extensions of his New Orleans world, at the other end of North America and at the other end of this journey, was a success; a farewell to the continent whose exhilaration at dismissal was as strong as the earlier voyage had been desperate. In "A Winter Journey to Japan," [8] really about Canada, Hearn's technique is resilient because he hopes for nothing and thus finds everything. He presents what is probably the seemingly fastest voyage across country ever recorded because he gives the sensation of speeding along by train through a series of cold Canadian landscapes by the use of rhythmically parallel impressions and prose.

Impressions come with the blankness or the startling vividness of their immediate appearance. The first section ends with the sleepy realization of a beginning—"I feel the train rushing through the darkness; the long journey has begun"; the second grows with clearing awakeness, and both the order and the shape of the perception are correct: "Morning. Heavily snowing out of a heavy gray sky. White·drifts line the way. Beyond them, on either side, is a waste of low growths,—young black spruce and dwarf birch—straight as lances; the silvery bark of the birch, strongly relieved against the somber spruce, gives their leafless shapes the aspect of poles stuck in the snow."

The eyes adjust to detail, the mind responds with greater agility, the prose reflects this reaction in its complexity. In even sentences Hearn sketches the long day, broken only by clusters of yellow houses or by a hazy wave of far-off mountains, and the brevity of this chapter for the day accommodates the vacancy of its experience. The next day begins with the blurred perception of a hypnotic, pale sun; and it continues in broken-up language to describe the vast lake frozen with isles and promontories, dotted with Indian names, scarred with open cliffs, slashes of trees. The first long pause—Winnipeg—produces a halt in the current of his descriptions; suddenly there are people aboard the train, aware of their warmth; he has time to calculate and compare, to note that at Winnipeg it is twenty-five degrees "below zero, with a strong wind blowing from the north."

For the seas of the Canadian prairies he has an undulating, repeating language:

. . . all this universe of snow has been wrinkled by the wind;— and the edges of its furrowings, catching the sun, flash like foam-breaks;—and under all the milky wavelets are wide, long undula-

tions like tide swells: the whole seeming to billow and flow by the
delusion of our motion . . . and our train sways like a vessel upon
some smoothly heaving sea; and the rhythmical thunder of its
rolling . . . and the long white-sprinkled track across the waste
. . .[9]

Under the jagged Rockies we have crowded paragraphs of rocks,
and snow, and spruce, and peaks, and clefts. Even the bridge high
over the Fraser is abstracted—and suspended prosodically in the
middle by dashes; everything written about across Canada is calculated for effect. Hearn has finished his American experience by
demonstrating his mastery of the rhythms of the American language. At the Pacific this long, breathed sigh of relief is over; the
final pages start to lose control, begin to drag or appear confused
or unplanned—Hearn is starting to head out for the Indies again,
only this time the Indies are Japan. Having demonstrated his self-
confidence in "A Winter Journey," he loses it once again.

CHAPTER 5

Japan

1890 and the last journey: Lafcadio Hearn renews his explorations
of an unfamiliar world, still the American reporter in search of
sensation. This time the subject is Japan, but the manner is that of
the same traveller who went to the tropics—the impressionist, the
sociological amateur, the folktale gatherer, the willing student of a
disappearing culture. But the monologue is longer; collections
based on the model of *Two Years in the West Indies* now come
forth for the English-speaking world almost regularly. They are
done on the same French principle, that, if the collection as a
whole has a certain *ambiance*, a congeniality, the important critical fact is the nature of the individual piece. Although Hearn's
overall production is greater, the number of really memorable
pieces remains the same. Here and there in the expansive volumes
are moments when his now old and practiced talents find a subject worthy of their skill. He goes to Japan, travels and resides in
a wide variety of circumstances even for Japan; acquires a Japanese wife and her family; becomes a schoolmaster to young Japanese students; immerses himself in studies of Japanese custom
and belief—but remains a thoroughly Western writer.

For Hearn's early Japanese years are simply the re-created experiences of an outsider; he is an eccentric one but American in his
eccentricities. With the utmost devotion to his waiting audience
across the Pacific, Hearn's literature does not disturb the expectations created by his handling of New Orleans and Martinique.
Technically, in fact, nothing new happens; so far as *development*
of his talent is concerned, the period from *Glimpses of Unfamiliar
Japan* (1894) to *Gleanings in Buddha-Fields* (1897) is uninter-
esting. Indeed, only the current of Japanese novelty alone suffices
to keep Hearn from being boring. Perhaps his style shows some
tendency to be less obtrusive than it had on some other occasions:
but that does not mean that it is always more subtly effective. The
one noticeable trend in these four early collections is *impersonality*

—even more than previously and with even less reason (than, say, the cub reporter for Cincinnati newspapers). Hearn makes himself a means, a camera, an interviewing machine. But he rarely finds the locale which balances so much personal effacement.

I   Glimpses of Unfamiliar Japan

Glimpses of Unfamiliar Japan,[1] eight hundred pages long, is really twenty-seven pieces joined, as before, by various devices. The subjects are the figure of the children's god Jizō, the loss of Japanese innocence at European hands, of Japanese elegant simplicity versus lavish Western vulgarity, of the Japanese "national soul" or "racial tendency," of contrasts and interchanges between Buddhism and Shintō, and, ultimately, the place "never before seen by European eyes." Hearn's approach is deliberately naïve: "I do not think this explanation is correct; but it is interesting. . . ."[2]

He continues his Creole-period practice of throwing in Japanese words while we wait for the explanation of the term in its natural occurrence; but, as usual, he often assumes that we will recollect its meaning from its context in another essay. As with the Creole Negroes, we are amused with his superstitious blather about "racial impulses" in the forefront of his discussion of Japanese superstition; yet he has shown a creditable attempt, once again, to learn as much as he can through the most advanced interpreters of Japanese culture.

And, like the West Indies pieces on travel, the Japanese travels are largely ephemeral, lovely successions of trifles like some Sunday-afternoon television travelogue, or worse, useful only as a guidebook to witless itinerants. The "inner life" of Japan, for which the preface lays a claim, scarcely exists; only "The Japanese Smile" can really be said to strike below the surface. The wise reader of *Glimpses* follows, therefore, the warning in the title and alerts himself to wait for those scattered moments of life by which confidence in Hearn's art is restored.

Most fragmentary of all these fragmented sketches, "My First Day in the Orient" (3–34)[3] appears at first to be a hasty collection of notes; instead, it is really an unconscious self-portrait of the impatient, curious, West-hating, impression-seeking, slightly hesitant, intellectual-sentimental new arrival. The only unity lies in the narrator—thereby, he becomes the story. It sketches the traveller and his enthusiasm, not the travel which inspires him. Of the fourteen actual travel pieces, only two, "In the Cave of the Children's Ghosts" and "At Mionoseki," stand on their own as appreciable units. The rest are just plausible, tolerable contexts for brief flashes of brilliant description.

In "Jizō" (41–71) there is a sensitive, vivid reconstruction of the appearance—coloring, atmosphere, inhabitants, their expressions, gestures—and more, the story, of the Hell Scrolls. By the use of his old technique of *recurrence,* the narration of an object frozen in time, Hearn uniquely perceives the scroll paintings within the conventions of Oriental art. His narrative succession parallels the eye of the instructed beholder:

> Floating in glory, Dai-Nichi-Nyorai, Kwannon-Sama, Amida Buddha. Far below them as hell from heaven surges a lake of blood, in which souls float. The shores of this lake are precipices studded with sword-blades thickly set as teeth in the jaws of a shark; and demons are driving naked ghosts up the frightful slopes. But out of the crimson lake something crystalline rises, like a beautiful, clear water-spout; the stem of a flower—a miraculous lotus, bearing up a soul to the feet of a priest standing above the verge of the abyss.

Sometimes his scene-setting is notable for its restraint and its careful placing of objects in sequence, with an eye to poetic effect: "A furnace, with souls for fuel, blazing up into darkness. Demons stir the fire with poles of iron. Down through the upper blackness other souls are falling head downward into the flames."

In "A Pilgrimage to Enoshima" (72–120) it is not the total visits to two shrines which count, but three theatrical moments—the sounding of the bell of Engakuji; the vision of the monstrous statue of Emma, the god of the Dead; and the revelation by lantern-light of the statue of Kwannon. This last scene depends upon the narration following the adaptations of the eyes in a darkened temple; the performance of sensing the great height, the expectations set up by the realization of the presence of a golden foot, the slow raising of the lanterns by rope, and especially the unexpected but logical step beyond the head to the crown of faces—the telling reinforces the excitement of the experience.

A cataloguing pattern, usually a dependable warning to the reader to skip several pages, near the end of "At the Market of the Dead" (121–38) is exceptional. First of all, it follows Hearn's

progress through a market place; second, the listed things are ac-
companied by descriptions of their use or action or by details of
their construction; third, an amiable pattern of street-calls is used
to introduce each article. In "The Chief City of the Province of
the Gods" (161–99) the final segment of nighttime sounds and the
interplay of light and shadow reflects the moods of the watcher by
the window frame, and thus becomes more than mere description.

A separable part of "Kitzuki: The Most Ancient Shrine of
Japan" (200–44) quite fails in its purpose of "getting inside" the
religion of Shintō, but succeeds admirably in conveying the bewildering meaninglessness of the formalities of a strange religion.
This visit is to the Great Man, the High Priest of the Shrine; the
Shintō rigmaroles make little difference, for the foreignness and
the gracious sweetness of a formidable being are the real topics.
By his surroundings, the guidebook-impersonality of the priest's
talk, the historical contexts within which Hearn sees the priest, the
virgin who dances for them, the small politenesses of the priest as
private gentleman—by these things Hearn creates a portrait of
the priest.

From "At Hinomisaki" (317–30) we would remember the suggestive and keen description of the friezes and of wood-beamed
temple construction. "From the Diary of an English Teacher"
(103–71) we would want to preserve the reports of days when
Hearn allows the realism of his material to contradict the sentimentality of his narration—or his sketches of the characters of five
students, each one with a style peculiarly suited to his personality
(the forceful one even begins to take over Hearn's narration!).

Despite Hearn's apparent effort to be polite in his recollection
of his first day on the payroll, the whole scene has an air of ridicu-
lousness, which is brought to the surface in the governor's odd
citation of the even odder reason for Shintō handclapping—a reason which is unscientific and irrelevant, amidst all this pseudo-
modern efficiency. Again in the classroom, the polite assistance of
his colleague Nishida is absurdly equated by the ingenuous Hearn
with the obviously drill-like rising and bowing to command by the
rows of uniformed students around the room. The quaint essays
Hearn has collected displace the earnest appreciations or moral
probings he has just tried to see in them. The reality, which he
gives to us, contradicts his enthusiasms, and is thereby enriched.

"From Hōki to Oki" (242–324), finally, erupts into life when
Hearn assumes his old role as clown: the scenes on the over-

loaded, stifling boat and those of a European curio in a village hotel are Hearn at his hilarious best. All the gymnastics and crowding of the curious village people wild and thick as they are, trying to stare into his room, are carried on in a deathly silence, which makes their tumbling even more bizarre. Comedy, intense objectivity, portrayal: these qualities we know already as Hearn's talents; when they are given a chance, they illuminate the wasted, lengthy letters home that surround them.

The very falseness of "In the Cave of the Children's Ghosts" (245–66) (Hearn has eliminated the presence of his wife, changed a relatively happy excursion into a somber afternoon) ensures its superiority. Its two settings, the "compressed" town of Mitsu-ura and the cave itself, are united by the idea of children: children's ghosts and the brown, naked lovely children of the sea-village seeking to watch the foreign visitor. There are two moods, fearful and a delighting charm; there are two kinds of coloring: black for the terror, yellow for the absurdity of the town. In the first half, persons are ugly, threatening, weird, incomprehensible; in the second, picturesque, innocent, pretty faces. Even where the images are old ones, "rocks rise around us like black teeth," or the techniques are familiar ones: *"Though-we-look-at, Thing-that-by-looking-at-is-worn-out-it-is-not!,"* the effects would be grim or the scene would be funny without such expanded emphasis. And, for once, Hearn's speculations on the transitoriness of impressions (and smiles) are neatly corroborated by the subtle ease with which his story moves from one mood to the other.

"At Mionoseki" (267–82), a lighthearted, thoroughly agile piece, begins and ends with gay Japanese songs. The whimsy associated with a god who hates chickens is utilized to emphasize the brutal efficiency of the modern world impinging on this sheltered village, a world symbolized in the vast metallic imperial gunboat. The work starts with mock (and attention-grabbing) severity: "The God of Mionoseki hates eggs, hen's eggs. Likewise he hates hens and chickens, and abhors the Cock above all living creatures." That this idea is no pious appreciation becomes clear with Hearn's observation that in another small village the same legend is used to rationalize the wholesale killing of chickens. The village scene, in which Hearn makes a playful request at the inn for eggs, ends in a joke on him: duck's eggs are served.

After a lull with temple visits (obligatory to Hearn as a travel-ler, but here functional), we turn to the sailors of the small harbor craft: ten naked oarsmen and their song, their "rough" version of Japanese gentleness at night in the taverns. Then the gunboat arrives, and childlike villagers are invited aboard. Refused a promised trip, their pitiful regrets are spelled out by Hearn in his word-for-word—but all the more ingenuous—Japanese English. The stalwart, indifferent marines are atop the decks, and the scattering of the endangered craft around the huge cruiser could create disaster: "if the cruiser were to move now there would be swamping and crushing and drowning unspeakable." It does not do so in fact, but Hearn, who has completed the suggestion of disaster, contemplates "the magnificent horror of . . . the multiple enginery of death," the nightmares paid for by millions of humiliated farmers.

But before Hearn's temptation to preach carries him over the brink of inattention, he switches back to the "delightful" relief of the town and to its silly god who hates eggs—only allowing himself a final, reminding twist in the last sentence, that on board that man-of-war there probably *were* eggs; and this time the god of Mionoseki is too weak to punish the disrespecters. In this way Hearn's story returns to its tone of humor but one tinged with the sadness of a lost world. We supply the meaning; Hearn only sighs in the manner of his repeated whimsy—"and, oh! Koto-shiro-nushi-no-Kami, there probably existed eggs on board!"

"Shinjū" (331–39) is another piece which starts brilliantly— "Sometimes they simply put their arms round each other, and lie down together on the iron rails, just in front of an express train." This opening not only is startling (and unidentified) action, but is the savory combination of the old and new Japan which is the focus of his essay. Hearn puts forth Schopenhauer, and then defeats him with the simpler reasons of the Japanese themselves for their own suicides; gathers the customs and causes of *shinjū;* and ends on an actual love-suicide experienced by Hearn in Matsue, complete with document. The suicide note from the girl to her employer is the sole fictional reality of the piece.

Like "Shinjū," "Kitsune" (358–94) is informational, a traveller's sociological notes put forth with a care for intellectual satisfaction. Brief, consistent, credible, the slanting and simplification are quite unobtrusive. A hodgepodge of fox-stories, "Kitsune," Hearn points out, merely conforms to the impossible confusion of the fox-beliefs themselves. But the placing of each tale is done finally with close feeling for the development of succeeding moods: a mood of smug learning, of historical curiosity, of skepticism battered with testimonials, of the cruelty of mischief, of cruelty and mischief combined, of credulity, of relief in the form of farce, of hilarity with an undercurrent of pain—and last, a tribute to the cleansing power of Western scientific education which, after the calculated sequence of tales, seems somehow right. The point of this and "At Mionoseki" are opposite; but both convince largely without argument.

Hearn is also, in this collection, the traveller who listens to roadside peddlers, to old inn-gardeners, to the quaint beliefs and tales of the local yokel. His travel stories are decorated profusely with such garnerings; occasionally, though, we come across some folk legends which stand on their own in the midst of larger narratives—and, as we might expect, the tales usually fall into the categories of *zombies* and hatred revolutions of his old American interests. In "The Chief City of the Province of the Gods" two street-locale tales detain our notice, and they are old favorites—the love-in-death theme, the ghosts with an unreasoning persecution of the living. In "By the Japanese Sea" [4] we detect the weird put to work again to promote the vividness of the tales, which are at once eerie and sentimental: a woman watching her husband and brother drown, the children whose ghosts haunt the wearers of their quilt. All this leads inevitably to the last piece in the collection, "Of Ghosts and Goblins," [5] where only one fragment—a tale of a girl who puts each of her lovers to the task of eating a corpse—produces in the old, grisly manner the chills promised by the title. The rest of "Ghosts," being travel or intractable plotted material, is merely diverting.

II Out of the East

Out of the East [6] is not even tolerably amusing. Not even fragments of fragments are to be found to light the way between long passages of colorless description. This work is much shorter, eleven sections, and about two hundred and fifty pages. As if embarrassed by the failure of *Glimpses* to penetrate the "inner life" of Japan, *Out of the East* drifts more and more toward perilous philosophic incontinence—or, worse, toward pseudo-Buddhist frauds upon his American public. As logic the pieces are reprehensible, as reporting they are insufficient, and as literature they are merely boring. This unfortunate habit we have already seen in his

works during the years at New Orleans; like other traits, the habit
continues as Hearn plays the American in Japan.

But in this volume, for the first time, the reporter starts to serve
the propagandist; and the artist begins to serve the bigot. These
roles nearly ruin the next two volumes as well, *Kokoro* and *Gleanings in Buddha-Fields.* In an environment Hearn does not know,
with a people he cannot understand, unable to read in their literature, and barely able to communicate with them, Hearn is a fool
to neglect what he can see and feel before him and to attempt to
penetrate and explain *real* Japanese life. He is particularly foolish
since he, alas, had no talent for history or ideas to begin with: in
New Orleans he took Herbert Spencer as his prophet—because he
so misread and distorted Spencer that Spencer spoke to him of his
own previous intuitions. In Japan he takes Buddhism, the attractive "religion of millions," and misreads it stupidly and willfully so
that it too speaks *to* him with the voice of Spencer and, behind
Spencer, with that of his own preconceptions. If Hearn created a
response in America by these studies in "Synthetic Buddhism" (at
least he was that honest), it is largely because he chose to see an
American and Victorian Buddha. Nothing could be more ironic,
therefore, than the image of Lafcadio Hearn as the artist who
deserted his country for Japan.

Perhaps the growth of these yearnings for philosophic distinction has some connection with the way in which these scenes of
Japan in *Out of the East* begin to reveal the hardness and brutality underlying the "layers of silken" politeness which had so capti-
vated Hearn earlier. Increasing restlessness and nostalgia, a dull-
ness and monotony reported in the landscape itself, start to show;
and even the students do not inspire him to glowing portraits of
charming individuals. "With Kyūshū Students" (24–53), on the
contrary, presents an anonymous mass of sullen, arrogant ene-
mies, their compositions full of sententious commonplaces or mechanical and melancholy ideas on life. Hearn provokes them into
writing naïvely on lofty subjects; they respond cruelly with dismal parodies of his own disconsolate loneliness and feeble speculation. As they yearn patiently for the lost sentimental days of
their childhood, so their teacher, Hearn, longs with nostalgia for
his year in the old Japan at Matsue far to the north.

The stories, the folklore researches, the travels, the descriptions,
the speculations have the *formal* virtues of his older perform-
ances; but the initial choice of the subject for which he will use his

art lacks care. "Bits of Life and Death," "A Wish Fulfilled," "The Stone Buddha," "The Eternal Feminine," "Jiujutsu," "The Red Bridal"—all are adequate, even informative; but none is memorable. Their abstract preoccupations merely underline their basic, melancholy distraction.

"The Red Bridal" (186–214), for example, is an attempt to dramatize facts Hearn has reported elsewhere in the volume: love suicide, arranged marriages, children's thoughts. But the story has only one real personage, the scheming peasant-woman, O-Tama; and her character is almost smothered under a heap of moralizing abstractions about her actions and psychology. The children in love remain silly story-children, even in their love-death. And Hearn himself, who steps in at the climax to puncture the effect with a much livelier tale of how a policeman had once detected his foreigner's eye peering through a hole in a shoji screen far above a street, demonstrates both his lack of interest in the tale he is supposedly relating and in the greater liveliness of his own life.

Or, "The Dream of a Summer Day"[7] is purportedly an arrangement of two tales: in the first, Hearn elaborately connects details to modern Japan—the boats, the damnation-period for turtle-murder, fashions in hair-styles, husbands and wives still rowing side-by-side, the imperial annals. But even more prominent than this practice of inserting contemporary references, which keeps the story at a distance, are the anachronistic nineteenth-century tremors of philosophy with which Urashima contemplates the empty box before him. Only the grisly, sudden, spasmic ending recalls the old Hearn. In the second tale, once we have made our way through chapters of murky revery or dry external biography, all the irony is spoiled at its beginning by overdevelopment of the point of the tale. That these stories might have been interesting we can readily testify; but Hearn has rudely dealt with his subjects by overemphasis upon settings.

III Kokoro

The third collection, *Kokoro*,[8] shows a revival of energy, if no advance in artistry. As the title suggests ("heart"), Hearn is still striving for that elusive "inner" Japan, a vain quest which vitiates more than half of the fifteen pieces. The increasing stultification of Hearn's stories, or the waste of his time in didactic speculation, is compensated for by works which are good *despite* his intentions. The remarkable thing about "At a Railway Station" is how little difference would be made by placing the story in Cincinnati or in St. Pierre. Its stark reportorial honesty in depicting an emotion-laden scene, combined with restraint upon both musings and sentiment, inevitably recalls Hearn the sensational newsman.

The first section is preparation: brisk and businesslike announcement of the striking news event. Then paragraphs of retrospect increasingly close in on the scene at the station—Murderer Confronts Victim's Child. The second section is horror-pity: first, an uneasy anxiety is set up about the crowd; then this is contradicted; and, finally, the contradiction is withdrawn. Then come confusion and terror for the criminal, for the child forced upon him, for the breathless "crowd" in tears at the brink of violence. In the third section, a musing replay of the scene, the abstractions serve merely to reinforce the deep emotional quality of what has been seen. The fourth section shifts the mood to relief, the Japanese love of children.

But the closing paragraphs turn this pious appreciation back to the plane of a child's terror amid horrifying, bloody desperation: its goodness amid the most criminal indifference to life. By describing the crime—"seven persons had been literally hewn to pieces while asleep,"—rather than the child looking on, we are reminded of the implication—that the child had been left to watch, uncomprehending and terrified; and that this crowd is enjoying repeating the brutality. That is, in trying to demonstrate Japanese compassion, Hearn's drive for realistic terror demonstrates instead a much more likely harshness and lugubrious self-indulgence in the people. He is making the Japanese very much like the Americans he had already described in the Cincinnati and New Orleans newspaper columns.

Two pieces of war reporting are also exceptions to the rule against Hearn as sociologist: "After the War" and "A Glimpse of Tendencies." [9] "After the War" has the peculiar advantage of reporting that *presents* rather than explains, and Hearn himself is sometimes revealed as he confesses his unease at the trumpet sounds of war (the calls of bugles form a motif throughout) because they suggest the sorrows which go with victory. This piece is unusual, too, for its prophetic objectivity about the brutal course of Japanese patriotism (it would be pleasant to stress this foresight were Hearn not so blatantly enthusiastic about Japanese chauvinism in other essays).

"A Glimpse of Tendencies" also finds an emotionally divided and therefore less didactic Hearn. Its theme is the decline and obliteration of the foreign options in Japan; but the sketch is particularly vivid in its exploitation of nationalist madness and will. Once again Hearn is strikingly prescient: he senses war, military dictatorship, internal disorder, and suspension of the constitution. Indeed, he seems to find himself so far departed from his intended delight that he makes a perfunctory try near the end to reassure himself and us that, nevertheless, the old Japan has a superior "sexual morality" (!) and a finer sense of "duty" than the West could provide—surely an egregious case of seeing Western ideals in Japan and then forgetting that the West ever gave the author such ideals.[10] But the vivid contradiction of his own claims survives the impression made by these remarks, the fact outdistances the opinion; and we may admire his reporting for that reason.

Again, by betraying Hearn, we may save him: the mood of "In the Twilight of the Gods" (423–32) seems intended to inspire indignation—but the characterization is so helplessly rich (in the old New Orleans' Creole fashion) that the eccentric outargues the well-intentioned interviewer. The conversational tone of the opening section (abrupt, colloquial) is never lost, even in the idle speculative meanderings of the narrator, which are treated contextually, mental distractions from which he is always pulled back. Without overdoing the description, he conveys the effervescent, indifferent, insensitive *delight* of the commercial museum-piece collector—a vulgar sacrilege whose very joy is its own excuse. We should especially note the way in which Hearn hates to disillusion the dealer (backslapping, pointing, chortling) about the "cross-trampling" devils, as if he too could not bear to destroy so much innocent pleasure. He almost regrets not having provided London with an exotic thrill, however spurious it might be; even the vulgarity of the proposal to melt down the Great Kamakura Buddha seems somehow admissible since the dealer is clearly so confident, so eager to be appreciated, so cheery—and, moreover, won't really be melting down idols any longer. At the end, even Hearn is drawn into a vast, gaudy vision of all those warehouses of Buddhas in some manner "raising" the British, too. The contrasting motifs of quotation from Buddhist scripture, then, become simple irony: they are another form, as we see, of vulgar display.

Elsewhere in *Kokoro* we find the usual fragments within fragments: the memorable thing about "The Genius of Japanese Civilization" (270–93) is not Japan at all—it is a hate-filled description of New York as a monstrous inhumanity of wires, buildings, machines, vibrations, darkness. The unpretentious claims of "From a Traveling Diary" (300–17) are generally fulfilled by its increasingly faded contents, but the opening lines about Japanese faces as portable masks are worth stopping for—especially the paragraph on Hearn's accidental discovery of the real, inner face of his laughing old servant; it is relaxed into hard "lines of pain and anger."

In "Kimiko" (498–512) it is not the artificial and lumbering plot which we notice; instead, it is likely to be the opening sketch of the darkened street of geisha-houses, its closeness, its strange lanterns, the lavish names, the endless corridors. Or we have the moment when Kimiko breaks out of the bondage of her author-enforced nobility to deliver a speech of coldly rapacious vengeance—but with the utmost sweetness of motive and meekness of refined Japanese pretension. The plot is predictable; not content with the "weepy" ending, Hearn goes on to destroy the credibility of what has been related: the father "tells no one" of what he has just seen. The ending is an attempt at rhapsody on Buddhist Truth —a sentiment quite at variance with the point of view, the tone, and especially the psychology of the story. Hearn, luckily, cannot quite force reality into the mold of his intellectual hobbies.

If he does succeed in "proving" Buddhism, he does so at the expense of literature. "The Nun of the Temple of Amida" [11]—the story of a bereaved mother who goes mad—is told as if the author knew nothing about either psychology or madness. Everything is taken at face value; but all the clues are also thrust at us: the insatiable sorrow, the child-spirit's confession of self-sacrifice, the old grandmother's comment, the mania for small things, the neighbors' counsel to their children. We know, as the narrator pretends not to know, that the nun is mad. Peculiarly, the sadness she is supposed to feel is never conveyed since she is treated like a happy idiot, seen from the outside. The sentimentality derives from this fact: *our* empathetic suffering, not hers, counts. During whole pages, indeed, she is unreal because she is on exhibit for quaint customs, songs, and journeys. If the piece were realistic, it would be hurtful; as it is, it is merely cute.

"Haru" (347–54) is also terribly sentimental. This sentimentality arises from the self-indulgences of a bored, sensual narrator who tries to prettify every dramatic confrontation and every stark reality; that is, sentimentality stems from a falsity in the point of view. For example, we cite the death scene:

> caught the bosom of his silk robe *in one quivering little hand*
> and looked into his face with eyes *that seemed to search for some shred of soul*
> she fell. He sought to lift her. But *something in the delicate life* had snapped.
> much running for doctors. But she lay white and still *and beautiful*

The italicized details are gratuitous observations made by the palpitating narrator, and are distractions from and contradictions to the pathos of the scene. In the closing and earlier sections, the narration is so clearly abstract-summary that we are not annoyed by such authorial interference. Though one doubts his or her psychological authenticity, one accepts the emotional set-up, at least. In a dramatic scene, however, she appears to be putting on an act if we cannot attribute her perverse glamor to the cruel selectivity exercised by the author.

IV Gleanings in Buddha-Fields

The *Gleanings in Buddha-Fields*[12] contains eleven selections and is the last collection of works from the early Japanese period. "Synthetic Buddhism," that dubious creation of a weakening man, is almost irresistibly present, even in the literary or travel pieces. Had this writing been on Christianity, it would long ago have been dismissed as sincere but naïve pious maunderings, or as a vain effort to believe on the part of an alienated snob. These very excesses must have become apparent to Hearn, for he never again attempted to use his literary works for the airing of intellectual anxieties.

The story in the midst of "A Living God" (3–23), for instance, breaks out of a morass of information and comparative religious experience; but it is the sole memorable fragment. The characters are null, but the moments of panic when the sea runs away from the land—until Hamaguchi sets fire to the ricestacks—are presented in the most carefully executed rhythm of unease, hint, horror, and desperate search of memory.

"Ningyō-no-Haka" (97–102) avoids the sentimental temptations inherent in a child narrator by playing with the superstitions
that surround the family troubles. We note the humorous pathos
of the ancient grandmother's scolding her dead daughter for trying to drag off the grandson, or the willingness of Hearn to take
on the little girl's sorrow by daring the curse to take effect, a joke
on himself rather than a tearladen farewell. The girl's narrative is
economical, except for the key death-scene. Hearn's description of
her tone and its meaning as a triumph of emotional control becomes a clever device for achieving straightforward narration and
for getting us under her emotive spell.

At the center of "Out of the Street" (24–34) is a triple series of
translations from popular song-lyrics. As when in the American
tropics, Hearn, interested in the folkloric life of the people, is an
inveterate recorder and reteller of folksongs and folktales.[13] There
is necessarily a difference between the Japanese form and the
English reproduction; other than any barriers separating the two
languages, the fact simply remains that Hearn never gets beyond
a kind of baby-Japanese; he is always at a distance from the original. In "Out of the Street," for the varied five- or seven-beat
rhythms of the lines, he invariably chooses a roughly equal two-
line structure, but there is no other discernible prosody. In fact,
this rhythm is often awkward, even for his English. Compared to
the originals, his English versions are (as he frequently points out,
of course) much less simple and direct: there is a slight stiffness of
word-choice (particles, especially). The songs read, therefore, as
if he hadn't quite finished bringing them into polished English.
The result is not a poem collection, but a satisfactory impression
of the tone of Japanese popular songs in general.

"Buddhist Allusions in Japanese Folk-Song" (143–61) might
also be accepted on the basis of its overall impression; but these
Japanese songs are terribly flat: on the one hand, there are two
prose statements; on the other, there is overly diluted handling of
meaning and grammar. Nor do his literal translations (hidden in
the footnotes) work better; although he seems to see some of the
wit and cleverness in the more lively poems, he is not able to
transfer the knowledge from his notes and commentaries into
poetic English. He reads as if he had not been able to decide
whether these songs were to be treated as literary experience or as
religious annotations. But this dilemma, one of the artist versus the

sociologist, is a very good sign, as we shall see. Hearn's days, once again, in this locale were numbered—as they had been in Cincinnati, New Orleans, Martinique.

As if he were returning to the mood of the first travels in Japan, "Notes of a Trip to Kyōto" (35–65) carries us back to the mood and style of those happy, early days of discovery. Two themes run under all the accumulated impressions: how the Japanese have perfected those pleasures which are most evanescent; the influence of poverty on their concept of pleasure—pleasurable things are small, detailed, natural, ingenious . . . and cheaply acquired. We would scarcely suspect Hearn's underlying purpose on a first reading, so varied are the landscapes and the personages: the voice of a geisha, the beauty of lantern-styles characteristic to each street, the Summer Palace garden, toys and novelties, fragility and poetic simplicity in pleasure, procession-viewing, procession-viewer viewing, on small gifts. . . . The visit to the grave of the *chauviniste* is a little horrifying (caked blood on the knife-handle), but even here the Japanese eye for detail is noted in the journal of the distraught, fanatic heroine. And the effect, however incidental thematically, is to upset the good will developed around the concept of Japanese triviality.

The best fragment (in this collection of admirable fragments) is a Western-style restaurant where Westerners had never come—it is out of the way; the client ascends into it by a ladder, eats with the knives and forks of an abandoned hotel, and listens to a music box and its strangled performance. In this scene, unexplained and unexpected, Hearn himself demonstrates the validity of his themes: the visit, an unexpected and trivial pleasure, is a small and hidden oddity whose charm lies in its very accidental nature. The essay as a whole is performing, however, what it talks about: its fragments are the small, choice, evanescent pleasures which make Japanese life so seductive. The unobtrusiveness of this thematic unity is all the more Japanese; as Hearn comments in the course of the piece, "the greatest applause is silence." "Notes of a Trip to Kyōto" marks at last the merging of Hearn's artistic method with the countryside he has so long desired to capture.

Japan, inner Japan, had escaped his eager grasp until he had returned to the Japan of his senses. The long Japanese years had produced literary strivings more frequently fruitless than productive. Even the ultimate reconciliation at Kyōto was achieved with-

out an advance upon his New Orleans technique—and by means
of a return to his earliest, least ambitious approach to the Japanese landscape. Hearn had come full circle, from Tōkyō to Matsue
to Kumamoto to Kōbe back again to Tōkyō. But this time, the
country exhausted, Hearn the reporter could not escape.

CHAPTER *6*

Alone

IN the years before Lafcadio Hearn's death, Japan was his literary prison. Unfamiliar Japan had now become a too-familiar country; once again he climbed to the top of the land, contemplated what he had conquered, and was ready to leave. Married, with a large family of children and relatives, he could no longer pick up his light baggage and flee the landscape he had exhausted of inspiration. Now only one route of escape remained—inward. Partially, he returned to the past, to old notebooks, to old themes, to old visions, and, through these, he came closer to himself. The new turn inward was painful, perhaps very much so; for until now, Hearn the literary creation of Lafcadio Hearn the author had been "your reporter," a mask, an impressionable traveller, a scholar-researcher.

The gestures toward an inward exploration were sometimes veiled in the halting language of generalized deduction to be found in the published works and in the remains of his notebooks. The bad habits he had acquired, especially those of rhapsodic poems to the philosophy of Herbert Spencer (now attributed to Buddhism), evaporate and disappear. The suspended development of his literary art stirred, and moved forward again. He had at last attained the shores of that other country for which he had so long searched.

I *"Fuji-no-Yama"*

The final glimpse of the Japan that Hearn was putting behind him comes, like the glimpse of Cincinnati from the cathedral spire, or like the glimpse of the tropics from the top of Pélee, from the peak which both overshadows Japan and symbolically represents it, Fujiyama. This view, the culmination of Hearn's tradition of travel writing, is perhaps his greatest achievement in the combination of scene, rhythm, and meaning for effect. The first of all

the pieces in the eight final collections, it is the last important
gesture to the hopes and desires of his Japanese period.

"Fuji-no-Yama" [1] begins with a poetic epigraph and with an in-
troductory collection of facts, distant views, and quaint notions
about Fuji that initiate us as the narrator is currently being initi-
ated in preparation for the climb. The epigraph, especially in the
translation, uses an ambiguity to create a sense of disappointment,
of regretful frustration:

> Kité miréba,
> Sahodo madé nashi,
> Fuji no Yama!

> Seen on close approach, the mountain of Fuji does not come up
> to expectation.

We imagine, particularly when the piece opens by praising the
beauty from afar of the mountain, a "distant apparition," that Fuji
somehow betrays the impressions made in these dreamlike visions
upon intimate, material acquaintance. With this warning, the
mood is set for a betrayal. And the betrayal indeed occurs; but,
like the untranslated twist in the Japanese poem, it comes in an
entirely unexpected and beautiful manner.

Parts I to V form an extremely skillful evocation of the sensa-
tions of the pull up the mountainside. After beginning with a
short, impersonal glance at a line of waving towels or at the gray
rain—impatient, stationary motion—the author turns to the double busyness of dressing, of lasting the noisy night, of the arrivals
of breakfasts and bearers. The next pages convey distance and
motion without any struggle: short paragraphs, flowing ellipses
between leisured sentences, degrees of light, passing silhouettes or
high roofs or tree clumps through the fog, the crunching sound of
black cinders on the road. The observer is held within a haze, and
his position is defined by the objects which intrude themselves
upon him from the morning darkness. Fuji is saved, thus, for the
sunrise vision: the mountain is blue, *warm*-blue; has luscious
curves; is "a woman's shoulders." It appears, delicious and entic-
ing, just before that very illusion has to die.

Part II is a thematic contest between black and green. The
landscape reveals more of its nightmare; the mountain, still a
spectacle, grows blacker and blacker, a "naked black reality"; the

snow patches are eventually like the gleam of teeth in a blackened
skull, or like a woman's skull burnt to a crisp. Part III insists upon
the loneliness of the travellers: only once, at a distance, do we see
another pilgrim, aside or atop the mountain—otherwise we see
just the cast-off sandals like the traces of a vanished population.
We become aware, too, of the way in which stations mark off the
stages of the trip. Here, in this section, the metaphors turn to ge-
ometry; with increasing steepness, the curves of the slope become
shot-lines. Humor is used alternatingly to emphasize the contex-
tual starkness. Silence and grim reflections are broken by the
guides' reproving Hearn and his "honorable nose." Hearn's religious awe of the "artificially" smooth edge of the landscape is dispelled by the guide's simple description of soft sand.

But in Part IV, as the breathing and the struggle become
harder, the funniness disappears; the guides only have time to
shame him; he has time only to hear them as part of the noise and
his embarrassing weakness. The sentences lose pronouns, articles,
and are in gasps—the flavor is increasingly envious, ashamed. A
motif of stones comes forward: shapes, sounds, looseness, malevo-
lent recalcitrance, threats. The spurts of upward motion fall into
paragraphs, more and more strange and abstract as the climbers
get higher; and there are the silent fall of rocks behind one where
one dares not to look down, and snow in massy, hard globules.

In the fifth section the night's rest cabin is attained; Hearn
slumps onto a couch, then restores himself and the fullness of his
language by eating. And then he turns around for the first time to
take in a vision of Japan beneath him, a transformed world. Here
is the climax, the true meaning of the poetic proverb at the beginning—the unexpected horror of Fuji and the equally unexpected
beauty of the entirely unknown world left behind. The revelation
takes on an almost metaphysical quality: a re-creation of the
world as a hollow sphere; the horizon, a luminous equatorial zone;
the lonely man on Fuji at the very center of a universe. The disappointment—indeed, the terror of the mountain—is the means by
which one can make the rest of the world beautiful.

Later on, beside the huge dead crater, windswept and hideous,
words come to Hearn to express this paradox: ". . . these—seen
through the haze of a hundred miles—through the soft illusion of
blue spring weather—appear as the opening snowy petals of the
bud of the Sacred Lotus! . . . No spot in this world can be more
horrible, more atrociously dismal, than the cindered tip of the

Lotus as you stand upon it." And he completes the disillusion which creates illusion: "But the view—the view for a hundred leagues—and the light of the far faint dreamy world . . . all this, and only this, consoles me for the labor and the pain. . . ."

Parts V to VII are in effect the descent, though the men are actually climbing to the top. One sign is the repetition of the intuitional paradox at the crater-edge: now it is only intellectually spelled out. Already the rhythm of description is beyond struggle to attainment. The seventh part even states the nature of his descent; and the sixth part is the story of a rescue, and in it tone and language alike belong to relaxed contemplation after the vision has been won. Fuji does not live up to expectation: it tears away the mask of beauty from itself, but it transforms the rest of the world. There is no deep truth here; but there is a deepness of experience which makes the paradox esthetically satisfying. Hearn creates in prose the tightly suggestive equivalent of the *haiku* with which he began.

II   *Insects and Poetry*

Such artfulness with the literature of travel makes all the more puzzling Hearn's apparent inability to respond to the wit in Japanese poetry. During the course of most of the final eight volumes of his literary career—*Exotics and Retrospectives, In Ghostly Japan, Shadowings, A Japanese Miscellany, Kottō, Kwaidan, The Romance of the Milky Way,* and *Japan: An Interpretation*[2] —Hearn was a collector of insects and poetry, usually in the same piece since one was the excuse for the other. As we have already noted in the last chapter, what is curious is that he never found a means for conveying in an English statement the peculiar, artful combination of sensation and wit so characteristic of the short Japanese poem. For a man so aware of the potentialities of the order of impressions in a story to be so indifferent to the order of brief ideas in a poem is incredible; and yet his translations (or, since he was always publicly modest, even distressed, about his "equivalents," his *prose transcriptions*) almost inevitably lose the thrill which he himself analyzes deftly in his notes. None of these anthologies of poems and insects[3] have more than a mild and pleasant taste to them; they are catchalls for a kind of mania for small objects and for Hearn's avid contemplation of them. They are the result of a successful obsession—they do not reveal Japan; Japan is instead ransacked in order to reveal Hearn.[4]

He typically presents the poem in two or more lines of prose: "Faint in the moonshine sounds the chorus of insect-voices: To-night the sadness of autumn speaks in their plaintive tone." In "Bits of Poetry" he insists vividly upon the necessity of the poet's leaving the matter *incomplete* in his poem: "the term 'ittakkiri'—meaning 'all gone,' or 'entirely vanished,' in the sense of 'all told'—is contemptuously applied to verses in which the verse-maker has uttered his whole thought. . . . like the single stroke of a temple-bell, the perfect short poem should set murmuring and undulating, in the mind of the hearer, many a ghostly aftertone of long duration." Yet most of his versions in the same work are one or two flat, completed sentences:

Moonlight on the Sea

O vapory moon of spring!—would that one plunge into ocean
Could win me renewal of life as a part of thy light on the waters!

Happy Poverty

Wafted into my room, the scent of the flowers of the plum-tree
Changes my broken window into a source of delight.

The more literal and fragmentary he becomes (and this happens only occasionally), the more highly suggestive is his English version. For example, we have this famous poem from "Frogs": "Old pond—frogs jumped in—sound of water." The implications of Bashō's contrast between the still, ancient water and the momentary, lively animals is particularly resilient in Hearn's brief resurrection because he chooses the option of making *frogs* plural and then of reverting to the singular for the delicate balance in the last line, an absorption of life which is also a response and a symbol of fleeting action. Or there is this "mere thumb-nail sketch" from "Bits of Poetry":

Furu-dera ya:
Kané mono iwazu;
Sakura chiru.

'Old temple: bell voiceless; cherry-flowers fall'

There are the reverberating strokes upon a canvas which Hearn describes in the originals—not the bland, finished English water-colors he ordinarily gives us.

Many of the *haiku* (17-syllable) and *tanka* (31-syllable) rely for their power on the order in which the impressions are received; and in this respect Hearn's carelessness is most regrettable. The form of the short poem is often like that of a joke: it has the unexpected twist which is revealed as perfectly just. If the punchline comes first, how is one to be startled into thoughtfulness? In "Fireflies," Hearn has abandoned his parallel prose and his "behold-whither" English; but, even when he has a simple speech and phrasings capable of arrangement, he stumbles:

> Owareté wa
> Tsuki ni kakururu
> Hotaru kana!

Ah, [the cunning] fireflies! being chased, they hide themselves in the moonlight!

How easy it would have been to reshuffle the parts, to trick and then delight the audience:

> Being chased,
> they hide themselves in the moonlight!
> Ah, [the cunning] fireflies!

Foolishness is after all wisdom; and the progression is from illuminated background to seen-and-unseen tiny foreground glow—but only if we have the wit to tell the poem as a joke.

An equally clear instance with a parallel point can be found in "Dragon-Flies":

> Onoga mi ni
> Aki wo soménuku
> Tombō kana!

O the dragon-fly!—he has dyed his own body with [the color of] autumn! [5]

If we reshuffle, the poem has both the picturesque red dragonfly and the suggestion of extravagant fashionableness:

> His own body
> he has dyed with [the color of] autumn!
> O the dragon-fly!

The connoisseur's delight in a suite of reflecting reds, and the completion of an equation between visual rapture and animal hunger—is it a bird's moment of esthetic perception or is it a poet's vision of his own flickering desire?—these are possible suggestions left to the reader in:

> Tombō toru
> Iri-hi ni tori no
> Métsuki kana!

"To hold a dragonfly in the setting sun" or "to eat a dragonfly at sunset": whichever it is to be, the red dragonfly comes first, and the look in the eyes comes last—an inner contemplation contemplated. But Hearn shuffles it again to produce an entirely foreign suggestion—a world of angry reds:

> O the expression of that cock's eyes in the
> sunset-light—trying to catch a dragon-fly!

Sometimes the metaphoric conceit in the original is so powerful that no amount of disorderly indiscretion can obscure it. At these moments, Hearn's translations seem honest: "O the thin shadow of the dragon-fly's wings in the light of sunset!" or "O the face of the dragon-fly!—almost nothing but eyes!" In "Frogs" we find the poem, "Even the rowing boats can scarce proceed, so thick the clamor of the frogs of Horié!" In "Sémi" we find, "Methinks that sémi [cicada] sits and sings by his former body—Chanting the funeral service over his own dead self," or comically, "The voice of the sémi is bigger than the tree on which it sings." In "The Romance of the Milky Way" the mythical star-god in his eagerness to join his beloved across the River of Heaven makes an emblem for lovers on earth: "Perhaps this evening shower is but the spray (flung down) from the oar of Hikoboshi, rowing his boat in haste."

Hearn's experiments with form are temporary; he inevitably returns to statement (later on, however, he hides his English in brackets, accentuates the *romaji* [roman-letter] versions of the Japanese). The few attempts at a three-line form are happy, as in this *haiku* from "Sémi":

> Matsu no ki ni
> Shimikomu gotoshi
> Sémi no koë.
> Into the wood of the pine-tree
> Seems to soak
> The voice of the sémi.

Occasionally the phrase-patterns of the English suggest a three-fold structure: "What I took for the falling of rain is only the singing of frogs." Only in collections made without regard for either topic or antiquity does Hearn find the best combination of form and language: a verse rhythm which arises out of the parallel grammar or out of patterned refrains. The "Songs of Japanese Children" vary from the commonplace or dull or confused to the charming or suggestive or even surreal; but they are usually real English verse.

> Evening-burning!
> Little burning!
> Weather, be fair to-morrow!

In the following, even without the visual arrangement, one is aware of the rhythms in the original:

> Sleep, sleep, sleep!—For the little one who goes to sleep, a
>   battledore and shuttlecock!
> For the child who does not sleep, only a shuttlecock!

In the "Old Japanese Songs," too, the irregular forms of ballads, dancing songs, and love lyrics—and the very simple substance—encourage Hearn to use English forms that attempt to look like a poem. We cannot imagine the following poem, for example, in the shape of continuous prose:

> My darling boy!—
> Oh! they have sent him to the rice-fields!
> When I think about him—
> When I think,
> When I think,
> When I think,
> When I think . . .

Such uninhibited play seems possible only when Hearn is un-
aware that someone might take his caprices seriously.

Among the hundreds of poems very few can stand being taken
by themselves as individual lyrics. The butterfly *haiku* which he
calls "tiny colorsketches . . . pretty fancies, or graceful suggestions," the *haiku*, nostalgic and sensuous, which he elsewhere calls
"picture poems,"—these decorate the interiors of his collections of
insects, and they merge into a sweet over-all expression. But they
do not any longer redeem themselves as poetic intermediaries. If
they did once, for the dissatisfied young poets of the turn of the
century,[6] we can only remark that most of these transcriptions,
those from the sophisticated tradition, lacked the poetic heart of
the originals and their intricate structural wit. From all those hundreds, we would want to rescue only one or two:—"Ah! the lost
child! Though crying and crying, still he catches fireflies!"—because they have the artful denial of their own sentiment that all
the best *art nouveau* designers have been producing, and not because they are Japanese.

That peculiar obsession of Hearn's, insects, and especially himself as an insect, does not do much for these collections of information, citation, allusion, and whimsy about insects. The closest
we come to entertainment in these grabbag anthologies, heavy
with cataloguing, are a few uneasy jokes. In "Gaki" bugs are metallic monsters—"the lips that are hands, and the horns that are
eyes, and the tongues that are drills; the multiple devilish mouths
that move in four ways at once; the living scissors and saws and
boring-pumps and brace-bits. . . ." In "Gaki" and in "Mosquitoes" Hearn transforms himself with lurid glee into various insects, but the performance is only brief, a grisly farce in a stuffy
museum. There is oddity enough in the desire to be "able to run
and to slide upon water" when it includes the possibility that
"children might catch me, and bite off my long fine legs." But this
is a whimsy, like the desire to become a mosquito and bite certain
people; and we still know too much about zoology and too little
about people who think themselves into bugs.

Blah, of course, continued to pay. As an American writer,
Hearn continued to turn it out for his public. But, by and large,
these pieces were only an occasional lapse of his usual good taste.
One volume, *Japan: An Attempt at Interpretation*, is no more
than a collection of lectures he intended, cynically, to give at Cor-

nell University; and then, equally cynically, he decided to publish
these wearily dated works since he was stuck with the manuscript
and badly needed money. *Kwaidan,* on the other hand, contains
no lectures at all. One piece of reporting in the posthumous *Romance of the Milky Way,* "A Letter from Japan," is another example of Hearn as a war reporter. He uses his visual experience of
everyday Japanese life to convey the feeling of seething military
devotion, even in a survey of toys. But this piece is exceptional:
most of the inspirational-educational-mystificational tracts are just
Blah.

III   *Translated Tales*

Translation, like bugs and poems, is a familiar Hearnian oddity.
But at the end of his life Hearn goes on technically with translation from where he had left off long before in New Orleans.
Ignorance of Japanese, perhaps, forces this evolution upon him.
He relies upon his *Herunsan* dialect with his wife and with his
relatives and servants, and upon word-for-word English transcriptions from his readers; he sends his wife out to see plays and
buy old books to re-enact for him; he pumps his aged samurai
father-in-law; and he drains the resources of his student assistants
—but he acquires the lines and figures of Japanese story.[7]
And this very innocence he makes a virtue: on the model of his
late translations from the French, of Villiers de l'Isle Adam and of
Zola, he proceeds to make the Japanese texts the pretext for a recreated tale which comes as much from himself as from the pony
which his wife or his archivist made for him. The reconstruction is
implicit in the process of making a new, English story; but Hearn
does more: he weeds and prunes, he exaggerates and undercuts,
he frames and disproportions. He pushes translation to the very
limits of tolerance. Chapters, incidents, persons, adjectives are undeniably Japanese; yet Hearn has the power always to make the
fiction insidiously his own.[8]
These translated tales are Hearn's own principally because they
are about obsessional subjects. Again and again he retails the narratives of horror, of monstrous superstitions, of lurking ghosts and
vengeful lovers. If the awkward interlanguage versions do not belong to a dark world of the nightmare or the irrational, Hearn
pushes them aside; nothing will do but an objective mirror of his

own subconscious terror. Just as the helpless, musical insects have some appeal for him which he could not analyze and which he could not avoid exposing in his constant collections of them, so the nightmarish tale is the one way in which he had always been able to enter the half-world of his own dreams: sex, death, the exotic unreal. He tells students, "Trust to your own dream-life; study it carefully, and draw your inspiration from that. For dreams are the primary source of almost everything that is beautiful in literature which treats of what lies beyond mere daily experience." [9] Here, in the last years of his life, he did the opposite: he told and retold the story of his inner life in the form of someone else's dreams.

The language of his later literature of the ghastly is severe; the place is ostensibly Japan, but local coloring is parsimonious; and form follows function in the cold sensational style of Maupassant. The thrill, the tension, the awe—the emotion alone counts. And since nothing is allowed to distract from it, everything is neatly at its service. The vast majority of his later works are translations of this peculiar order, and the large majority of the translations are dark, death-ridden, and full of the odor of malevolence.

There is an ambiguity in Hearn's relationship to his stories; often he interrupts and distracts the reader from the mood of foreboding he has worked so hard to erect, as if he were undergoing a sudden revulsion to his own experience of fear. In the "Story of O-Kamé," [10]—otherwise a rather smooth relation of the jealousy of a dying wife and the slow draining of the husband by her ghost—at the end when the long-dead corpse is exorcised, Hearn as narrator abruptly emerges to make a wry, cynical comment: "But whether he always kept his promise, the Japanese story-teller does not say." As much as to say, I really doubt whether chastity long remembers terror.

In "Furisodé" [11] the story is considerably insulated, by both the personal and the pedantic remarks in the frame paragraphs and by interruptions in the narrative which have the appearance of showing off (". . . of the Nichiren sect . . . an old custom to . . ."). In "A Passional Karma" [12] the story is framed in two short incidents that confront the narrator and a friend whose personality is best described as knowledgeable indulgence; and this frame has the effect of counteracting the horror in the tale, especially the little trick of politeness played on Hearn by the potato-patch woman. Instead of the tombs seeping with the perfumes of Romanticism which he is looking for, the narrator finds himself only in realistic and obligingly spurious human relations—and does so in a potato patch.

As Hearn tells us during the story, his method of translation is close only "in the conversational passages" because they provide the most "psychological interest." "A Passional Karma" is, therefore, an abridgment, but one with a nasty purpose. The early incidents of the story are rapidly narrated. Shinzaburō's grief and the women's battle to gain him form the lengthily told portions. Motifs—of the sound of women's wooden shoes, of the weeping of O-Tsuyu—lead to their slowly apparent pursuit of the weak, cowardly Shinzaburō. O-Tsuyu's weeping covers an unyielding passion; its repetition suggests an insatiable passivity, culminating indeed with her strangling embrace. Shinzaburō's delicate, despairing leisure also signals his openness to possession: "Clad only in a light summer-robe, he sat there thinking, dreaming, sorrowing;—sometimes fanning himself; sometimes making a little smoke to drive the mosquitoes away."

The most hair-raising scenes are preannounced but revealed so that the relaxed reader is all the more startled: we know, for example, that the servant will see Shinzaburō with a ghost, but we do not know that he will see Shinzaburō's body being caressed by fingers of naked bone. The most curious thing is that the horror of the story seems to cater (as do the pages proportionately) to the weak desire (without any personal involvement) of Shinzaburō, especially after his fear breaks out, "foolishly peeping," for the long-dead corpse who is sucking away his life. So it is all the more brutal to be suddenly deprived of his point of view during the love-death climax. All we see is his agonized face and, beside him in the bed, the bones of the dead woman he has been loving and who still has him strangled in her embrace. The priest in the concluding sections is rather pompously and selfishly omniscient amidst all this suffering and perversion, coming out too late with his advice and his tranquil denials. His presence (and emphasis) makes the story's tone not only horrifying but annoying as well.

A close comparison of Hearn's work with one of his sources quickly reveals the insistent manner of his transformation of Japan into his personal dream world.[13] "Of a Promise Kept" in *A Japanese Miscellany*[14] derives from a tale in the *Ugetsu Monogatari,* the work by the great eighteenth-century writer Ueda Akinari. A tale of devoted homosexual love, Hearn has stripped away the first third of it to give it an entirely different coloring.[15] Gone are the sketch of the noble family, the story of the compassion of the young hero, the tale of the warrior he restores to life (with its evocation of war and betrayals), the mother's adoption of the hero's new friend, their happiness, and in that joy the warrior's revived desire to return once more to his own country. Gone also is the ironic frame which Akinari builds around the fiction—a sarcastic moralizing on human inconstancy—and the poetic motif of the flowers of the seasons. Everything which would distract from the supernatural will to return is discarded; everything points toward the charging of the moment of incredible terror.

The young Hasébé's desire to know when his adopted brother will return from Izumo, the opening of Hearn's story, is not a demonstration of love but a long proprietary request: "Your Izumo—the Country of the Eight-Cloud Rising—is very distant. Perhaps it will therefore be difficult for you to promise to return here upon any particular day. But, if we were to know the exact day, we should feel happier. We could then prepare a feast of welcome and we could watch at the gateway for your coming." Akana's answer is supercilious, "suppose we say. . . ." The decision to meet at the festival of the chrysanthemums is elaborated and indifferent; it is not, as in Akinari, tender, brief, delightful.

Both versions skip rapidly to the day of the chrysanthemums, but the original lingers far more over the painful passage of time for Hasébé as he, waiting in front of the gate, uses bits of conversation from the strangers who go idly or hurriedly by to reinforce his silent distress. The poetry of the mother's proverb, as she tries to persuade her son to give up the watch into the night—"if there is no autumn in the heart of a man, will the blooming of the chrysanthemum-flowers last only a day?"—is beautiful because it calls on the imagery of flowers and season and because it sums up the theme of devotion and love. But the proverb becomes economical, indifferent, perhaps even flippant, when Hearn replays it: "The mind of a man, my son—as our proverb declares—may change as quickly as the sky of autumn. But your chrysanthemum-flowers will still be fresh to-morrow. Better now to sleep; and in the morning you can watch again for Akana, if you wish." There is smug skepticism in that final "if you wish."

Hasébé waits alone in the night until the moon begins to set. Where Akinari says, in the original, " 'It has been enough,' and turning to go back in and close the gate . . . ," Hearn has, "Then at last he began to doubt and to fear. Just as he was about to

reënter the house. . . ." Elements of terror, not pain; of the startling, not the lingering—these are stressed by Hearn.

In the conversation between Hasébé and Akana one key change
is made: Akinari has the ghost reveal his death at the start, but
Hearn holds it off until the moment of his departure. In Hearn,
Hasébé interrupts the explanations of Akana so that the amazing
feat of the one-day journey is emphasized: " 'Until today!' ex-
claimed Hasébé in bewilderment;—'the castle is more than a hundred ri from here!' " But in Akinari the tale of Akana's imprison-
ment by the cruel Tsunehisa could not be interrupted because the
teller was building up through his distraction to a recounting of
his suicide and to a sentimental farewell, tears from his ghostly
eyes. All the speech was focussed on the irony of the cost of their
reunion: "Now our separation will be for ever." No tears and no
poignant phrase mar the progression of Hearn's prose toward a
different focus—"Then Hasébé knew that Akana had killed himself in order to fulfill the promise." Undermotivated, weird, his
death is realized by the hero just as it is revealed to the reader.

Again, at the end, Hasébé's grief; his proof of the vision to his
mother; his farewell to her, with the underlying flavor of life's
evanescence; his despair behind his angry vengeance—these aspects do not interest Hearn and so do not appear in his story. A
whole page of abuse of the treacherous nobles of Izumo is expressed by Hearn in the word "reproached." The new last section
exists only to restore the breathless reader to the realistic, complacent world in which he had begun.

Not all of Hearn's translations do so much to rescue a dream
world out of an existing fiction. In a second tale from the same
Ugetsu Monogatari, for instance, the story is more immediately
responsive to Hearn's needs. "The Dream Carp" [16] becomes "The
Story of Kōgi the Priest"; but, except for the title, the two versions
are much the same. Hearn has only tinkered here and there to
change irony to seriousness, or to produce more amazement. In
the opening part, the priest does not merely paint the fish he pi-
ously rescues from the boatmen; he goes so far as to hire boatmen
to catch them for him, the serious artist. His refusal to sell the fish
paintings is no witty rebuttal to his admirers, but a painter's indignant rejection of mere money. The key word "jokingly" is twice
ignored in two sentences: "hito-goto ni tawamurete yū, 'Shō o ko-
roshi azarakeki o kurō bonzoku no hito hoshi no yashinau uo
kanarazu shi mo ataezu' to nan: sono e to wazagoto to tomo ni

ame-ga-shita ni kikoekeri." We end, in Hearn's version, not with his fame as raconteur and artist but with his righteous restraint: ". . . but he said that he would not sell a picture of living fish to any one who was cruel enough to kill or eat fish. And as the persons who wanted to buy his paintings were all fish-eaters, their offers of money could not tempt him."

After the priest is revived from his trance by the disciples who had nearly taken him for dead, he tells an extraordinary story. In both versions the delightfulness of this man-become-fish is in the mixture of human and fish psychology by which he recalls his underwater experiences. His sunlight joys, his attraction to bait, his weaker fish-reason allowing him to yield at last, his indignant terror on the cook's chopping block: Hearn and Akinari alike have mastered the subtly ambiguous language needed in such shadowy recollections. Hearn makes the priest a somewhat more vivid person by introducing asides, disclaimers. He summarizes the priest-fish's tour of the Eight Famous Places without losing any of the moments which illuminate the nature of the fish-man.

Kōgi's terror under the knife of the cook is broadened by greater scene-setting in the kitchen, by squelching of the irony of his cries, and by emphasis upon his helpless assumption of a role he no longer wants ("I am not a fish!—I am Kōgi—"). Where Akinari says merely, "tsui ni kiraruru to oboete" (finally I felt myself being cut), Hearn insists on the drama: "in the same instant I felt his knife dividing me—a frightful pain!—and then. . . ." Nor is there any more playful ridicule of the pretensions of human reason; for the unravelling syllogisms of Akinari, Hearn substitutes the overpowering force of being physically a fish. In small ways like these, Kōgi the priest is changed from human eccentric to human victim.

So it is appropriate that at the end Kōgi does not, following his humor, let the fish out of his pictures back into the lake; nor does the author enter the page with a joke as to why no one has ever heard of such a marvellous painter. We stop a few sentences beyond the end of Kōgi's tale, seeing Kōgi paint a little more; and then, Kōgi already long dead, his pictures "happen to fall" in the lake and the fish-spirits, too, swim away. Hearn chooses the quiet way out for a story that he has made serious and only wistfully amusing. By and large, this subtle rearrangement of a ready-made world is the format of Hearn's late work in translation.

In each of the better translations a nightmare is to be expected. But there is a smaller subgenre which also appeals to Hearn—the tale of marvels. Hearn's manner is particularly appropriate to this category because neither he nor the originals have much liking for plot. The main raison d'être of the tale of marvels is the *effect;* the story exists to bring out simple amazement in us, nothing more. We experience awe, and the story is ready to end. Nothing else, not even character or theme or process, is necessary. At any longer length than Hearn's customary brevity, these tales would be intolerable; even within his dimensions, they probably fail to captivate a modern reader. In nine of the tales in *Kwaidan* alone, Hearn's essential technique is to construct a setting and social milieu around one or more odd incidents.[17] Actions and manners are often unaccounted for, but extensive credentials may be given for the strangeness of the events. Occasionally, we wonder about the narrator's relation to his own story; it is as if he had gone out of his way to undo its sole reason for being, its effect.

In "The Sympathy of Benten," [18] the story oddly disturbs its narrator on the least expected grounds—how, he complains, did the girl feel as a phantom and whatever became of the double? The effect is that Hearn hadn't the slightest idea of the conventions of a wonder tale—even in the West we do not inquire into how it feels to be a genie or into the private life of fairy godmothers. In "The Screen Maiden" [19] the narrator interrupts three times at a high point in the suspense to discuss some detail of translation, and these interruptions so fracture and arrest the story that its primary value—as a wonder evoker—is scarcely possible. The young scholar's passion is broken off, the séance is blundered into, and the appearance of the spirit is twice frittered away.

"The Story of Kwashin Koji," [20] however, is exceptional: its assorted wonder-tale incidents are bound together by the personality of the white-bearded entertainer-magician and in the equally framing series of persons from the age of the self-made dictators and their ugly treacheries. Alone, the incidents would sustain attention: a disappearing picture, the slain resurrected, the thief tricked into stealing filth, the murderer who cuts off a head and finds it a gourd, a painted lake which floods into a room. . . . What is best about the tale, however, is that the tone is always both humorous and weird; and the story does not insult our mental capacity.

At the beginning of *Shadowings* Hearn places a significant poetic epigraph,

> Il avait vu brûler d'étranges pierres,
> Jadis, dans les brasiers de la pensée . . .
>
> EMILE VERHAEREN

The best of the translations are like these strange stones of the quotation that burn in the braziers of thought: they burn because they correspond to some inner pain and inner vision of Hearn who reports them to us. They derive from the New Orleans *Fantastics;* and Hearn uses Japan as Poe might have used Italy. We have only to look at Hearn's titles to see how much he knew what he was collecting from the literature of Japan: *Ghostly, Strange Shadowings, Kwaidan (Strange Tales), Kottō (Curios).* Lust, death, hatred, paranoia, anxiety, necrophilia: all the old equipment of a Hearnian nightmare are present.

"Ingwa-Banashi" [21] releases a totally unforeseen horror in the middle of a tender, grief-stricken, even morally touching series of scenes—a brutally obscene action erupts from the last, weary conversations of a dying woman. At that point the narrative also speeds up, becomes economical; the old wife herself breaks into the colloquial ("why, this way!"). The possession of the new wife by the spirit of the first wife would have fulsome psychological connotations (lesbianism, hatred, jealousy). But the remaining tale of the poor hagridden second wife Yukiko twists the horror into nausea: the hands of the dead wife seared onto her breasts, the useless efforts to pull them off, the curse of the dried up and amputated claws still grasping her under her dress. The sexual-passional terror has been underlined with these emblems of disgust.

In "The Reconciliation," [22] another necrophilic romance, there is less fear of the dead because the fiction is constructed to put us at a distance. The element of surprise, upon which some of the incidents in the last sections could be expected to rely, is rather drained by the large hints provided in the entire page of descriptions of the decayed house ("a chilly wind was blowing through crevices in the planking," or even "the house, to all seeming, was unoccupied"); proportionately and explicitly, there is too much preparation. Even the corpse-punch is telegraphed: the husband sees the naked floor first in the morning, then the grave-sheet. Moreover, his superficial, self-seeking betrayal carries us away from his already less than startling horror towards a serves-him-right attitude. He is, due in part to Hearn, a rather sentimental slob.

There is suspense in the "Corpse-Rider" [23]: the title seems to give half of it away, but the half which remains is so classically sexual—the associations of riding, for example—that it has power enough to keep the story viable. The opening is harsh and utilitarian: short, sharp sentences set the mood of death and vengeance, *thus, thus, thus.* "The body was cold as ice; the heart had long ceased to beat: yet there were no other signs of death. Nobody even spoke of burying the woman."

The final guilty protests, which only make the scent of sexuality all the more redolent, are a peevish attempt to counteract the indecency of the tale. The wise-man in the story (the inyōshi) either is mystifying us or he is acting out a role of social-spokesman toward the trembling spouse. And we should note the psychological suggestion of the language: The inyōshi says, " 'You will have to do much more than look at her . . .' 'you promised' 'he forced the trembler into . . .' The husband remarks: 'quaking from head to foot' 'I dare not even look at her!' The description of the act: 'get astride upon her . . . sit firmly on her back, as if you were riding a horse . . .' 'take her hair in your hands . . .' 'never let go . . . she will tear you into gobbets.' The pain: 'till he screamed to break it. . . . ' 'Oh, how heavy it is!' " Suggestion is clear in the ride scene:

> Then tall she rose, and leaped to the doors, and flung them open, and rushed into the night—always bearing the weight of the man. But he, shutting his eyes, kept his hands twisted in her long hair—tightly, tightly—though fearing with such a fear that he could not even moan. How far she went, he never knew. He saw nothing: he heard only the sound of her naked feet in the dark—picha-picha, picha-picha—and the hiss of her breathing as she ran.

As if those rhythmic motions and repeating phrases were not enough, there is even an emblem for the postcoital exhaustion: "At last she turned . . . and lay down upon the floor exactly as at first. Under the man she panted and moaned till the cocks began to crow. Thereafter she lay still." We begin to understand Hearn's point about the usefulness of finding a world which corresponds to dreams. Once again there is much to be said for the American prudery which adds so much elegant repression to the dreams of desire.

Lust and death appear again in "Of a Promise Broken." [24] More than explicit foreshadowing, an at first odd and then ominous note in the series of requests on the dying woman's part—to be buried in the garden and to be given a little bell in the coffin—simply fulfills our taste (if we have stayed with Hearn's volumes of translations). The picture of the second marriage is quite rapid: no opportunity is given for the manufacture of sympathy. Then when the spectre arrives, despite its absurd speeches, the horrid appearance and the heavy immobility of the young wife nevertheless come through. Here the contrasting lengthiness of the dialogue between samurai and wife only serves to delay the horrible, to make it inevitable, to increase helpless suspense.

In the third section, at the peak of desperation, the point of view shifts twice: from the terrified young wife to the frozen guards; and then away from them to the samurai at dawn. And this ungenerous suspense has a calculated purpose—the horror is not the suspected one, but worse: the corpse still stands over the tomb, holding the head which we know has been torn off the body of the young wife. What had seemed a catharsis of evil in the dawn discovery is turned into an anticatharsis, as we are held more and more to the contemplation of the crumbling corpse and the dripping head, especially in Hearn's final poem of gore: "But the fleshless right hand, though parted from the wrist, still writhed;—and its fingers still gripped at the bleeding head—and tore, and mangled—as the claws of the yellow crab cling fast to a fallen fruit. . . ." At this point of revulsion, we are glad for the silly frame which is tacked onto the end: " 'That is a wicked story,' I said to the friend who had related it. . . .' "

In fact, as we read through these museums of terror, we can acquire habits through which the later Hearn tricks us into stupid curiosity and leaves us mocked by our own morbid sensibilities. Naturally, the tales of marvels and the ghastly visitors continue: "The Story of Mimi-Nashi-Hōichi" [25] has the usual hauntings, dark journeys, exorcisms, and disfigurings; but it is told with a kind of indifferent care. Only one section, that of the visit of Hōichi to the phantom court, stands out for its vividness because of its exploration of what a blind man's point of view means for a narrative of haunted experience (Hearn seems frequently to be attracted to oddly limited points of view). The ear-directed and hand-directed narratives give a special "reality" to the supernatural events, effects which have no visual substance.

But "In a Cup of Tea" and "Mujina" [26] are simply jokes on the reader that are within the conventions of the horror story. In the former, everything the narrator tells us about the story's not coming to an end is quite true; but we cannot expect so awkward a moment after the metaphors in the opening paragraph are so awesome, after the face-in-the-cup, the ghost samurai, the vengeful retainers—the rigamarole of wonders has to lead to some solution. But nothing at all happens; the tale ignobly grinds to a halt; the narrator emerges and dismisses us with the most insolent indifference.

"Mujina," a short-short marvel tale with a very solemn beginning, also turns into a joke. Just as the old merchant has escaped from the *mujina* (demon) with no face, arrives panting and gasping at the top of the hill by the side of a solitary noodle-seller, and tries to convey in broken sentences to this human companion his supernatural and terrifying experience, Hearn pulls down the curtain in full view: " 'Hé! Was it anything like *this* that she showed you?' cried the soba-man, stroking his own face—which therewith became like unto an Egg. . . . And simultaneously, the light went out." "Diplomacy" [27] also works this vein of countersuggestion. There is a great deal of realistic detail, a situation splendidly made for deathly vengeance, and then, no horror at all: the wise samurai has known from the start how he outwitted the ghost. And there we as readers sit, stupid and nonplussed.

In a very few of the last tales of the irrational, the dream world almost succeeds in triumphing over the real. Choosing the happy Chinese whimsy of "The Dream of Akinosuké," [28] Hearn makes the dream—because of its elaboration, its formality, its grandeur and legalism—almost a kingdom preferable to the outer, larger world of the dreamer. Only we suspect that the passing events of the happy sojourn exist so fully in order to emphasize the shortness of the "actual time" gone, and the pomp only to make more astonishing the "actual" insignificance in size—an ant colony. There is too much of the air of allegory around the tale and not enough of the magical.

If any reconciliation of Hearn to his dreams does come, it is in the choice of "The Story of Itō Norisuké." [29] The peculiarity of this tale is its calm—the hero fully accepts the ghostliness of his beloved (after a momentary chill), and her ghostliness in turn involves no emphatically cruel draining of him. His happiness and his peace with her elegance and beauty, not the slow death, are underlined. Even the interruption is a description of the awesome calm and dark of a midday, deserted Japanese village—and of why it should seem so. Even the learned quotation from Kwang-Tze—"their stillness was abysmal, and the people were all composed"—has the right combination of weird, ancient, silent, and satisfied tone for the following story. The feeling is: if this be illusion, make the most of it. The stress at the opening is put upon the hero's poverty. The condition at the end is the acceptance of the beautiful death to which he is yielding. A dream of acceptance is the last dream which Hearn translated into English.

IV *The Inner World*

Often in this period it seems as if Hearn were returning to forgotten or neglected sources of strength. Not only does he turn once again to reading to find himself, but it seems as if he were thumbing through old notebooks, trying to revisit old memories. In *Kottō* we find ourselves rereading "The Eater of Dreams," [30] a piece from the very end of his New Orleans work. The opening pages are like so much confetti falling to delude the listener into a state of only slightly uneasy amusement, before Hearn plunges into a revelation of horror. He climbs out from the terror by the same whimsical imagery, the same beast from folklore, almost reaching a clownish self-buffooning. He laughs and laughs as he begs the "eater of dreams" to rid him of this nightmare which has been so long haunting him; and, only if we know the Hearn behind this pose can we suspect that the laughter is forced.

The dream itself—no Japanese dream this time, but one publicly avowed as his own—has not changed very much. The corpse is there, so is the urge to examine it. He still notices its "unnatural" longness, still feels the fear of its eyes—as well as being devoured by it. And he again axes it into a bloody ruin, "the shapeless mass . . . of Myself." The use of powerful acts, the more powerful images, and the good old Hearnian rhythm of storytelling are present; but the language has changed from hysterical to weary. In "Stranger than Fiction" [31] he goes back to the West Indies, to

an unsuccessful theme of the forgiveness of violence, for the murderer is now a wasted old man who is followed by a troop of
chickens. And in "Vespertina Cognitio," [32] one of a group of *Retrospectives*, Hearn carries on the musings about himself at the edges
of a terrifying personal experience from Martinique. His analysis
is pitifully inadequate, but his atmosphere is beautifully convincing.

This contradiction between reality and the explanation of it, no
matter how desperate Hearn was for comprehension, never vitiates the truth of the experiences. Some of the rationalizings are
expanded versions of key ideas which move us when they emerge
in his stories—but in these personal sketches they are pompous
vanities, all out of proportion. He does not understand, evidently,
the real causes of why these incidents fascinate him; the stunning
personal materials, brought to the surface for the first time, utterly
ridicule the impoverished explanations he has found for them. Especially in "Gothic Horror," "Levitation," and "Nightmare-
Touch" [33] do we find theories which are quite unconvincing, disappointing, or completely incredible standing side by side with
embarrassingly naïve and lurid childhood memories.

Perplexity over the Freudian (to us) symbols in Hearn's awe of
Gothic churches is not really possible for us, as it was for him: he
locates the revulsion in the columns, relates them intuitively to the
naked palms of a tropical forest, paints their appearance as "monstrous, pale, naked, smooth-stretching . . . a life as conscious as
the serpent's"! What particularly annoys Hearn about the Gothic
column is a suggestion of "monstrous motion," the way in which
that life rushes toward the darkened groin above. Another vivid
moment in "Levitation" is Hearn as a phantom hovering at twilight, "trying to frighten lonely folk by making small moaning
noises"—what a statement of his literary bent!

And in "Nightmare-Touch" two childhood scenes objectify the
paranoia of an "appearance of secret conspiracy"—the terrible
helplessness of a child who is sure he is unwanted; a haunted
child, locked in his room by the forces of cruel Victorian duty, is
left to the tortures of inevitable goblins. The striking quality
about these memories is that they are as stunning as anything
Hearn has ever done in horror . . . and they are also frighten-
ingly realistic. His theories, that the common fear of ghosts is one
of being touched, could not be more absurd; but the illustrations

could not be less irrelevant. Hearn depicts the dream of every lonely child:

> I would try to escape (feeling at every step a sensation as *of wading*), and would sometimes succeed in struggling half-way across the room;—but there I would always find myself brought to a standstill—paralyzed by some innominable opposition. Happy voices I could hear in the next room;—I could see light through the transom over the door that I had vainly endeavored to reach; I knew that one loud cry would save me. But not even by the most frantic effort could I raise my voice above a whisper. . . .

These fragments, and those in the *Life and Letters*,[34] are the sole instances in which Hearn makes use of the dimensions of his conscious life in his literature. Certainly there are in his other works plentiful reflections of his dream existence (where the meaning is less gross and threatening) and frequent use of himself as a kind of camera, a kind of portable man-of-taste; but there is not this wrenching of material out of the depths of a life which has so fascinated biographers.

The posthumous fragments, starting with "My Guardian Angel,"[35] whether they are portions of an autobiography or the first sketches towards a new psychological realism (or, probably, both), are not always successful (being unfinished perhaps). But, when they are most personal, and least general, they demonstrate how powerful an author a Lafcadio Hearn in grips with reality might have become. *Might have become*—for the journey inward towards himself and towards a new fiction was broken off by death. If the dream, the fantasy, the exotic have previously provided the only way in which he confronted the inner hatreds and anxieties of his life, he seemed ready now to try to confront them directly. But he sorely lacked the intellectual equipment for grappling with them. Yet, as before in his career, if he had just contemplated them straight-on, without the benefit of explanation, we could fully react to them. His footnotes to the portrait of Cousin Jane may be wrong, but there is no denying that in a few pages she comes hysterically alive. He may have difficulty coming at the scene of "My First Romance," and his title may be gravely inappropriate from our perspective (even ironical); but the teen-age anger within his embarrassment and the despair within are conveyed neither sentimentally nor calmly.

Hearn has always had the ability to *see* clearly, so imaginatively
that we can share his hypnotic attention. This happens once again
at the opening of "Incense" [36]—

I see, rising out of darkness, a lotus in a vase. Most of the
vase is invisible; but I know that it is of bronze, and that its
glimpsing handles are bodies of dragons. Only the lotus is fully
illuminated: three pure white flowers, and five great leaves. . . .
I do not see the opening through which the radiance pours; but
I am aware that it is a small window shaped in the outline-form
of a temple-bell.

—but this time he is looking, not into a real temple, but into the
vision within himself. The lotus vase arises out of his own inner
darkness.

Hearn, who had always had the ability to let his prose convey a
sense of travel, returned in the last period to the early manner of
journeys to the seaside town. "At Yaidzu," [37] however, much built
into a pattern of waves of experience and memory like the waves
on its shore, is not a portrait of a town but of the narrator. In the
scene of the lantern-boats, it is his swim, not the boats into which
he peers, which is really "queer"; it is his meeting with the pale
figures of the landlord and his wife on the stony beach, their polite and quaint conversation, and not their little, contained story
which matter; it is Hearn's enthusiasm, his metaphors which
arouse respect, not the sublimity of his ideas. He is serious enough
about himself as witness and as *immediate* (not far subsequent)
philosopher that, in a minimal way, he starts to use event as he
had with General Forrest or Père Labat long before in order to
create the revelation of a man. This minimal, quiet side he is
ready to portray.

Attempts at something stronger than the tranquil or the clownish mask still break down or skitter away. "Vespertina Cognitio"
puts off the man terrorized by concentrating on the *ambiance:* the
heat, the smothering air, the scorching mattress, sweat like centi-
pede-feet, and night sounds like a wide, slow cataract of broken
glass. Somewhere within all that heightened sense-impression is a
man, but the man for whom Hearn has gone back to that West
Indies memory is not a man at all, but a funnel.

Up to its fifth page "Ululation" [38] is an excellent self-portrait of a peevish, terrified intellectual. In it Hearn uses the old rhythm of incident and description to peel off one protective layer after another from a man who, to begin with, merely cannot sleep because dogs are howling. But on the fifth page Hearn digresses with lectures and whimsies on evolution, sacred cannibalism, karma, and natural morality; he hides in the safe irrelevancies of abstraction. It, too, goes back for a technique, proceeds and then backs away from what it has done.

There is also a return to the sociological: "The Case of O-Dai" [39] is a tract hot off the fire of indignation. In this piece, even the cruel Japanese community suffers from righteous ire. The message is that unfilial East and unchaste West are equal absurdities, and that both societies are thoroughly revolting: "What becomes of the Japanese girl publicly convicted of offending against filial piety? What becomes of the English girl publicly convicted of unchastity? . . ." His irony lashes both sides, perhaps even outdoing his own intentions. The Enemy is there, drawn in the portrait of the two utterly obtuse, frigid, stiff old maids who happen to be missionaries; they turn aside the convert O-Dai on sensible, economic grounds and condemn her in willful ignorance to the sensible vengeance of her fellow Japanese. No matter how obscured by a collection of facts, the piece is not simply sociological: it is anarchistic hatred.

"On a Bridge," [40] in which Hearn returns to the earliest kind of naturalism, the most matter-of-fact tone with the greatest dispatch-like economy of words, seems starkly fascinating. The modifiers are all chosen to insist on extremes of objectivity: *here, from there, this much, in that order.* The only emotion in the whole of the peasant's story is in one sentence: "Then I saw that they were not peasants; and I was afraid." Otherwise the peasant contemplates both self and scene, oddly distanced from himself (for example, he simply reports that his body was shaking, not that he felt fear inside it). The quick description of quick action and the verbiage-free style might be compared with the style of a war story from Hemingway. However, Hearn has also gone back to his old device of a contrasting narrator from whom the control of the story is stolen: dense, an ignorant babbler who has to retract his protest sheepishly at the end, his pumping helps to accentuate the modesty of the old laborer, and makes us all the more conscious of the purity of the war scenes. What makes this piece a

part of the newer Hearn is that it is realistic terror, the terror of
war and not of ghosts, of fear in full daylight. As such, "On a
Bridge" is one of Hearn's best fictions.

But "On a Bridge" is not personal, even if its greater Naturalism
may result from an increasing reconciliation with the real world.
We have to look hard to find a piece which draws directly on
Hearn's mature life, and the nearest we come to it is the symbolic
"Kusa-Hibari." [41] The full bitterness of this very personal cry of
pain is apparent only when the epigraph is joined to the ending.
The epigraph "Issun no mushi ni mo gobu no tamashii" [even in
a one-inch insect a half is spirit] is *not* translated by Hearn; the
hatred remains hidden. The ending lines of the work show us the
agony of the singer but not the hatred. Only at the end do we
realize that what had seemed to be Hearn in the piece—the great
man, the god, the contemplative connoisseur, the sentimentalist,
the tyrant—is in fact the audience; and the true Hearn is the im-
prisoned cricket who at last eats his "heart" out because of the
hunger in which he is left: "Yet, after all, to devour one's own legs
for hunger is not the worst that can happen to a being cursed with
the gift of song. There are human crickets who must eat their own
hearts in order to sing." This is a harsh twist upon the conclusion
of a rhapsodic tribute.

And, like the twist at the end of a *haiku*, it causes readjustments
going back through the meaning of the whole piece, indeed going
back through all those strange insect collections. All the emotionalism of the story, all the self-indulgent regret for the accident
against the insect singer, all the virtuoso elegies just finished—all
are thrown in the face of the audience by the last words. The
epigraph, the hidden meaning, was literally "even in insects of one
inch, a half is spirit" and, proverbially a gesture of defiance: "even
the worm will turn when trod upon." It is pathos bordering upon
a resentment that suggests painful injustice. Hearn turns to his
living self to throw off the many roles, the literary guises, he has
assumed, and he comes up with a small symbol of that inner self,
a cricket.

Two years after "Kusa-Hibari" was published, Lafcadio Hearn
was dead. The journey towards the man within could not be finished. What remains of his work, therefore, is that great outer
voyage through the Cincinnati underworld, across France and to
New Orleans, in the islands of the Caribbean and Japan—and the

last embarkation towards himself through dream, memory, and symbol. He created fiction which approximates music in form, and art which rivals news in sensation. From beginning to end he was the reporter of unusual experience and the stylist who wished to make experience art. Within those bounds, his career was full.

CHAPTER 7

Conclusion

THE literary reputation of Lafcadio Hearn,[1] difficult to estimate on any count, has both gained and suffered from fad
and whim. In his last years, he benefitted in the West from the
first wave of fascination for the Mysterious East. As a conse-
quence, we can find the works of Hearn in family libraries all
across the United States, a testament of the enthusiasm of our
grandfathers. Thousands who grew up in that generation knew
and loved his writings. The great Pacific war with Japan in the
1940's seemed for a time to have obliterated Hearn from the
American consciousness, a kind of guilt over a youthful infatua-
tion. The misleading notion of Hearn as a spokesman for Japan
left him without literary defenses when Japan and things Japanese became the enemy. We might suppose, then, that the second
wave of fascination with Japan (which resulted from the occupa-
tion and the Korean War) would bring about a Hearn revival; but
this Japan of the 1950's was far different from the one Hearn studied. And besides, the two wars and the increasing world responsi-
bility of the United States had created a whole new generation of
contemporary interpreters of Japan like Donald Keene, Ivan
Morris, Earl Miner, and Edward Seidensticker.

Nevertheless, there has been an upturn in appreciation for
Hearn as a writer. And this time the re-evaluation seems more
honest and more accurate because it has come from an effort to
see Hearn as an *American writer*. Trying to place Hearn in the
context of American literature—whatever he may have chosen as
his subject matter—forces us to see two essential facts. One,
Hearn had been a disciple of the exotic since his youthful days in
Cincinnati; whether we call this quality the ghastly, the grotesque, the weird, or the sensational, Hearn began in America
what he customarily did in the West Indies and Japan.[2] Two,
Hearn never achieved success at the "major" genres of literature:
there is no corpus of drama, of poetry, or of novels left behind in

his name. Hearn was, and should be evaluated as, a practitioner of the smaller literary trades.

Hearn had a taste for the odd and the gruesome wherever he found it. He pushed on from Cincinnati to the South, from the South to the West Indies, and from the West Indies to Japan. Each was a locale which Hearn as writer used and then exhausted. He set out, as it were, to use the world as raw material for his American market. Only in the last days of his life did he begin to go beyond the assumptions he had made for his literary career while he experimented in New Orleans.

A balanced inspection of the literary work of Lafcadio Hearn sees his efforts as a whole, that is, sees Hearn as an American writer, whether on or off American soil. He is a part of the gothic tendency inherent in nineteenth-century writing; and, in this tradition, we should place him among the important figures of the second rank. But most characteristically American, he is that lucky immigrant so placed as to satisfy America's vast need for imitation, translation, and information about the outside world. Like many a guide, Hearn was not completely trustworthy, nor was he always amusing; but in the long run he gave Americans the sense of something new and different. His translations from the French are still being reprinted, and selections from his impressionistic sketches and travel writings are still valid enough in themselves to make their way into survey courses. *Chita* is a memorable work among the short novels of the symbolist period, and even *Chita* is not wholly original in form and mood. Accepting Hearn as neither prophet nor turncoat, we are able to come to a just estimate of his skills: he was a craftsman of the small and the impressionistic, but a craftsman just the same.

Notes and References

Chapter One

1. August 10, 1873, collected in *Barbarous Barbers and Other Stories*, pp. 29–36.

2. August 24, 1873, collected in *Barbarous Barbers*, pp. 21–28.

3. *Op. cit.*, p. 25.

4. *Ibid.*

5. February 15, 1874, collected in *Barbarous Barbers*, pp. 10–20.

6. *Cincinnati Commercial*, May 26, 1876, collected in *An American Miscellany*, I, 196–205.

7. March 8, 1874, collected in *Barbarous Barbers*, pp. 1–9.

8. March 1, 1874, collected in *An American Miscellany*, I, 1–12.

9. *Op. cit.*, 1.

10. *Cincinnati Commercial*, April 2, 1876, collected in *Barbarous Barbers*, pp. 172–85.

11. November 9, 1874, collected in *An American Miscellany*, I, 29–47. Also collected in *The Selected Writings*, pp. 233–43.

12. *An American Miscellany*, I, 36.

13. August 29, 1875, collected in *Barbarous Barbers*, pp. 201–10.

14. *Op.cit.*, p. 207.

15. January 23, 1876, collected in *Barbarous Barbers*, pp. 66–75.

16. January 7, 1877, collected in *An American Miscellany*, I, 214–227. Also collected in *Selected Writings*, pp. 250–59.

17. (Lexington, Ky., 1957). Six of these are to be found in other anthologies as well (*Occidental Gleanings*, *An American Miscellany*, *Barbarous Barbers*, and *Selected Writings*).

18. August 22, 1875, pp. 32–48.

19. March 17, 1876, pp. 61–83.

20. April 9, 1876, pp. 84–90.

21. June 27, 1876, pp. 9–12.

22. August 27, 1876, pp. 13–22.

23. October 1, 1876, pp. 23–31.

24. August 26, 1876, collected in *Barbarous Barbers*, pp. 220–37. Also collected in *Selected Writings*, pp. 203–14.

25. *Barbarous Barbers,* p. 228.

26. *Ibid.,* p. 237.

Chapter Two

1. And, through French versions, names like Dostoevski and Turgenev.

2. See especially Marcel Robert, *Lafcadio Hearn,* 2 vols. (Tōkyō, 1950–51), in this regard. There are more references to French literature than to English literature in his collected works. He admitted his ignorance of classical English literature: cf. the letter to W. D. O'Connor (*Writings: Koizumi Edition,* XIII, 322).

3. Robert, I, 55.

4. The translator is first critic of someone else's text: he looks into it for what he considers important to art. (A word-for-word criticism of translation, thus, shows a rather primitive conception of art.) Then he is a surveyor of English literary equipment: he must find or create some equivalent English techniques. A translator learns nothing, unless his reading of a foreign text coincides with his isolation of a new critical category.

5. *One of Cleopatra's Nights,* pp. 1–65.

6. *Une nuit de Cléopâtre,* in *Nouvelles* (Paris, 1904), p. 357.

7. *Nouvelles,* p. 350, and *One of Cleopatra's Nights,* p. 48, respectively.

8. *One of Cleopatra's Nights,* pp. 66–125. [=*La morte amoureuse*]

9. *Ibid.,* pp. 126–81.

10. *Ibid.,* pp. 204–21.

11. *Ibid.,* pp. 222–315. Other Gautier stories translated are "The Mummy's Foot," whose Pharaoh is treated with a similarly absurd familiarity (as if he were a suburban parent), and "Two Actors for One Role," in *Sketches and Tales from the French,* pp. 1–15.

12. Cf. Robert: "Par eux, le mot juste, le mot qui peint, l'agencement des phrases, l'élégance du phrasé, le charme des cadences, l'ordonnance des phrases en un ensemble harmonieux et chaleureux . . . lui deviennent une source inépuisable de problèmes, d'émerveillements et de soucis. Traducteur, il rivalise avec ses modèles d'exactitude et de souplesse." (p. 108)

13. New York, 1928. (The later editions have not been deprived of certain passages considered offensive to 1912 readers.) French critics have been complimentary: Robert calls it one of Hearn's best achievements as translator; Régis Michaud (in "Lafcadio Hearn et Flaubert," *Revue Germanique,* VIII [1912, No. 1], 50–53) calls it "digne du modèle et presque toujours heureuse."

14. *La tentation de saint Antoine* (Paris, 1924), p. 5.

15. *Ibid.,* p. 145.

16. *Ibid.,* p. 133.

17. Elizabeth Stevenson, *Lafcadio Hearn* (New York, 1961), p. 149, feels that Hearn's translations are "perhaps the best in existence."

18. *Saint Anthony and Other Stories* (New York, 1924), pp. 171–184. Hearn translations of twenty-three Maupassant stories appear in this volume; twenty-five more appear in *The Adventures of Walter Schnaffs* (Tōkyō, 1931).

19. *Contes et nouvelles* (Paris, 1956), II, 474 ("Un parricide").

20. *Saint Anthony*, pp. 113–22 and 125–33, respectively.

21. *Ibid.*, pp. 33–44.

22. *Ibid.*, pp. 261–71.

23. *Ibid.*, pp. 201–12.

24. *Ibid.*, pp. 3–14.

25. *Sketches and Tales from the French*, pp. 113–21. Also included are four other Daudet stories.

26. Daudet, "Le Curé de Cucugnan," in *Lettres de mon moulin* (Paris, 1894), p. 133.

27. Coppée, "L'invitation au sommeil," in *Contes rapides, Oeuvres complètes, Prose*, III (Paris, 1892), 5.

28. *Contes rapides*, p. 10.

29. *Ibid.*, p. 16.

30. Two collections, *Stories from Emile Zola* (Tōkyō, 1935) and *Stories from Pierre Loti* (Tōkyō, 1933), are devoted to these pieces.

31. *Sketches and Tales*, pp. 147–55.

32. *Ibid.*, pp. 19–20 and 23–30.

33. *Ibid.*, pp. 33–40.

34. *Ibid.*, pp. 43–52. Virtuoso, and faithful, translations of two other Villiers de l'Isle Adam stories are included as well.

35. Villiers, "Le secret de l'échafaud," *Oeuvres* (Paris, 1957), p. 379.

36. *Sketches and Tales*, pp. 187–96. (Extracts from the war chapter in *Le Calvaire*.) *Sketches and Tales* also includes a translation of Jules Lemaître's "L'aînée." *Life and Literature* (Tōkyō, 1925) includes a version of Baudelaire's "Les Bienfaits de la lune," a prose poem.

Chapter Three

1. *Occidental Gleanings*, I, 144–55.

2. *Ibid.*, 156–63.

3. *Ibid.*, 164–79.

4. *Ibid.*, I, 165.

5. *Ibid.*, 208–22. There are seven other "Ozias Midwinter Letters" to the *Commercial*, either in this collection or in *Barbarous Barbers*.

6. That is, aside from his humorous verse skits for the *Item*, and his various folk-song and poem translations.

7. Forty-five of them are collected in *Creole Sketches* (Boston, 1924). Of these, thirty re-appear in the Koizumi edition as "Creole

Sketches"; seven of these again appear in *The Selected Works*, pp. 260–83.

8. *Writings. Koizumi Edition*, I, 110–12. [All further page references in the text itself are to the appropriate volume of the Koizumi edition.]

9. Quoted in E. L. Tinker, *Lafcadio Hearn's American Days* (New York, 1924), pp. 78–79.

10. *Creole Sketches*, pp. 70–71.

11. Seven related Creole Sketches are to be found in *Barbarous Barbers;* three in *Occidental Gleanings*, II; ten in *An American Miscellany*, II.

12. The titles of the "Fantastics" have been added by the editor, C. W. Hutson. Those of the "Fancies" are Hearn's own. The same collection appeared earlier (Boston, 1914).

13. *An American Miscellany*, II, 16–21.

14. *Writings*, II, xv–xx, 1–94. Related sketches of a similar kind, not chosen by Hearn for this collection, can be found in *An American Miscellany*, II; *Karma* (New York, 1918); and *Occidental Gleanings*, II.

15. *Writings*, I, 209–99. Also collected in *Selected Writings*, pp. 89–132.

16. Hearn's version, as given in his notes, *Writings*, I, 289–90.

17. *Writings*, I, 1–100. Originally the subtitle of an intended collection to be called *Ephemerae*. Related to this collection is "Torn Letters" in *An American Miscellany*, II.

18. *An American Miscellany*, II, 66–73.

19. See the dreary collections in *An American Miscellany*, II; *Occidental Gleanings*, II; *The New Radiance and Other Scientific Sketches* (Tōkyō, 1939); *Buying Christmas Toys and Other Essays* (Tōkyō, 1939); *Editorials* (Boston and New York, 1926); and *Barbarous Barbers*, for just the New Orleans wastage.

20. *Writings*, IV, 143–257. Also collected in *Selected Writings*, 135–99, and alone, as *Chita* (New York, 1889, and in paperback, Greenwich, Conn., 1961).

Chapter Four

1. *Writings*, III, 3–111, and III, 113–390 plus IV, 3–141 (respectively).

2. O. W. Frost, in *Young Hearn* (Tōkyō, 1958), p. 212, gives fifteen different blues used by Hearn here, including "azure, ultramarine, pale vapoury blue, faint blue, spectral blue, foggy blue, pallid blue, limpid blue, gentian blue, ghostly blue, tender blue, flaming, dazzling lazulite, and ponded shades of diaphanous blue."

3. *Writings*, III, 28, 31–32, 48, 49. Cf. the erotic treatment of the boys in " 'Ti Canotié," *Writings*, III, 361–81.

4. See the discussions of "The Funeral of General Forrest" in Chapter 3 or even of "Porcelain Painting" in Chapter 1.

5. *Writings*, IV, 34–46.

6. *Karma* (New York, 1918), pp. 13–59. Originally it appeared in *Lippincott's Magazine* (April, 1890).

7. *Karma*, pp. 16–18 *passim*.

8. *Harper's Magazine*, November, 1890, collected in *An American Miscellany*, II, 243–65.

9. *An American Miscellany*, II, 249.

Chapter Five

1. *Writings*, V and VI.

2. *Writings*, V, 21n.

3. Also collected in *Selected Writings*, pp. 398–417.

4. *Writings*, VI, 187–210. Compare the "Chief City" tales to R. M. Dorson, *Folk Legends of Japan* (Tōkyō and Rutland, Vt., 1962), p. 97 and p. 216.

5. *Ibid.*, 337–55. Last literary piece, that is. Compare the tale reported in Dorson, p. 191.

6. *Writings*, VII, 3–261. The pieces in *Some New Letters and Writings of Lafcadio Hearn* (Tōkyō, 1925) seem to belong to this period.

7. *Ibid.*, 3–23. For the first tale, compare the version in Keigo Seki, *Folktales of Japan* (Chicago, 1963), no. 32.

8. *Ibid.*, 265–512. *Three Popular Ballads, Writings*, VIII, 357–418, belong to this period.

9. *Ibid.*, 330–46 and 355–81. The second is also collected in *Selected Writings*, pp. 521–36.

10. As Robert (*Lafcadio Hearn*, II [Tōkyō, 1951], 107) remarks, he always puts "l'Idéal oriental [contre le] *Fait* occidental"—and here, as often is the case, he doesn't really understand "l'Idéal oriental"; hence the trick appears to us, sixty years later, obvious.

11. *Writings*, VII, 318–29. In *Three Popular Ballads* Hearn confesses his sociological bias: the texts, he says, "from any purely literary point of view . . . are disappointing, exhibiting no great power of imagination, and nothing really worthy to be called poetical art."

12. *Writings*, VIII, 1–223.

13. Seki complains (vi): "But Hearn wrote down these eerie legends . . . in the mood of the mysterious East—exotic, occult, melancholic —rather than in the straightforward style of peasant storytellers." Yet Dorson, remarking that only Hearn gave serious attention to localized legends, jumps to his defense (29): ". . . those who dismiss Hearn as a dewy-eyed romancer should consider his grisly and macabre legends." This is two ways of saying the same thing—Hearn was an

energetic researcher without prejudices against "low" literature, but he was also an artist with pretensions to either *edification* or *effect*.

Chapter Six

1. *Writings*, IX, 3–29. Also collected in *Selected Writings*, pp. 429–444.

2. *Ibid.*, 1–210; IX, 213–71; X, 2–187; X, 193–397; XI, 2–155; XI, 159–267; VIII, 227–418; and XII; respectively. "Insect Studies," XI, 271–313, also belongs here.

3. "Insect Musicians," *Exotics and Retrospectives*, IX, 30–63; "Frogs," *Exotics and Retrospectives*, IX, 115–27; "Bits of Poetry," *In Ghostly Japan*, IX, 309–21; "Sémi," *Shadowings*, X, 45–69; "Old Japanese Songs," *Shadowings*, X, 110–36; "Dragon-Flies," *A Japanese Miscellany*, X, 241–69; "Songs of Japanese Children," *A Japanese Miscellany*, X, 282–344; "Heiké-Gani," *Kottō*, XI, 79–82; "Fireflies," *Kottō*, XI, 83–108; "Gaki," *Kottō*, XI, 113–27; "Butterflies," XI, 271–287; "Mosquitoes," XI, 288–92; "Ants," XI 293–313; "The Romance of the Milky Way," *Romance of the Milky Way*, VIII, 227–57; and "Goblin Poetry," *Romance of the Milky Way*, VIII, 258–89. "The Romance of the Milky Way" is also collected in *Selected Writings*, pp. 480–502.

4. In "Dragon-Flies," Hearn reveals an extraordinary passion to make Japan yield what he needs: "The friend who collected for me all the verses quoted in this essay, and many hundreds more, declares that he read through *fifty-two volumes* of thirty-one syllable poetry in the Imperial Library before he succeeded in finding a single composition about dragon-flies; and eventually, after much further research, he was able to discover only about a dozen such poems in tanka."

5. The brackets are Hearn's.

6. See Earl Miner, *The Japanese Tradition in British and American Literature* (Princeton, 1958).

7. See Elizabeth Stevenson, *Lafcadio Hearn* (New York, 1961), pp. 246, 249, 308 and 315 (but especially 246, where Hearn's correspondence to one of these helpers is quoted: " 'If I ask you to translate something, *please never try to translate a Japanese* IDIOM *by an English* IDIOM. That would be of no use to me. Simply translate the words *exactly*,—however funny it seems.' ").

8. For instance, Albert Mordell (*Saint Anthony and Other Stories* [New York, 1924], p. xi) recalls the plaint of one associate: "In fact someone who gave him the material for one of his later Japanese tales complained that Hearn introduced his own version in such a manner that it differed from the tale as originally told him." Moreover, all Hearn's "translations" were subsequently re-translated back into Japanese by admirers who often knew the sources.

9. *Talks to Writers* (New York, 1927), p. 149.

10. *Kottō*, XI, 25–29. Also collected in *Selected Writings*, pp. 382–395. Vengeful ghost-lovers, as Yu points out, are always female.

11. *In Ghostly Japan*, IX, 217–20.

12. *Ibid.*, 257–88.

13. He freely offers his sources, and it is often easy to find and consult them. Among them are the (Hearn's transcription): *Hyaku Monogatari, Jikkun-Shō, Konséki-Monogatari, Otogi-Hyaku-Monogatari, Ugétsu—Monogatari, Bukkyō-Hyakkwa-Zenshō, Yasō-Kidan, Shin-Chōmon-Shū, Uji-Jūi-Monogatari-Shō, Kokon-Chomonshū.*

14. X, 193–98.

15. "The Chrysanthemum Flower Vow" (*Kikka no chigiri*) is already a transposition from a Chinese Ming Dynasty tale, though with quite a different mood. The best available European translation of Akinari's tale is in *Contes de pluie et de lune*, ed. René Sieffert (Paris, 1956).

16. *Muō no rigyo.* "The Story of Kōgi the Priest" is in the *Japanese Miscellany*, X, 230–37.

17. "Oshidori," "The Story of O-Tei," "Ubazakura," "Rokuro-Kubi," "A Dead Secret," "Yuki-Onna," "The Story of Aoyagi," "Jiu-Roku-Zakura," and "Riki-Baka." All of these are also collected in *Selected Writings*.

18. *Shadowings*, X, 23–33.

19. *Ibid.*, 13–18.

20. *A Japanese Miscellany*, X, 213–24.

21. *In Ghostly Japan*, IX, 345–51.

22. *Shadowings*, X, 3–8.

23. *Ibid.*, 19–22.

24. *A Japanese Miscellany*, X, 199–207.

25. *Kwaidan*, XI, 161–75. Also collected in *Selected Writings*, pp. 23–31. The "Story of a Pheasant" (*Kottō*, XI, 34–37) is similar in its imbalance, creating a character—the husband—who is banished from the story after stealing the scene.

26. *Kottō*, XI, 7–10, and *Kwaidan*, XI, 205–7, respectively. The latter is also collected in *Selected Writings*, pp. 48–49.

27. *Kwaidan*, XI, 187–90. Also collected in *Selected Writings*, pp. 38–39.

28. *Ibid.*, 247–55. Also collected in *Selected Writings*, pp. 73–78.

29. *Romance of the Milky Way*, VIII, 312–28.

30. IX, 150–55. See "Three Dreams" in Chapter 3 above.

31. *Romance of the Milky Way*, VIII, 329–55.

32. *Exotics and Retrospectives*, IX, 193–204.

33. *Shadowings*, X, 149–56, 157–62, 163–72, respectively.

34. XIII, 15–23, 23–28, 33–34, 37–40, 41–44, 94–95. See also "Hi-Mawari" in *Kwaidan* (XI, 259–62), which has a biographical detail brought in almost accidentally.

35. In the *Life and Letters* (*Writings*, XIII–XVI).
36. *In Ghostly Japan*, IX, 221–41.
37. *Ibid.*, 358–71.
38. *Ibid.*, 299–308.
39. *A Japanese Miscellany*, X, 352–59.
40. *Ibid.*, 347–51.
41. *Kottō*, XI, 144–49.

Chapter Seven

1. See especially Malcolm Cowley's introduction to *The Selected Writings of Lafcadio Hearn*, ed. Henry Goodman (New York, 1949); Earl Miner's *The Japanese Tradition in British and American Literature* (Princeton, 1958); Elizabeth Stevenson's *Lafcadio Hearn* (New York, 1961); Beongcheon Yu's *An Ape of Gods* (Detroit, 1964); and the many works of pioneer Albert Mordell.

2. And this relates Hearn to the tradition of the American gothic, from E. A. Poe down to Faulkner and others today.

Selected Bibliography

PRIMARY SOURCES

The Adventures of Walter Schnaffs. By Guy de Maupassant. Ed. Albert Mordell. Tōkyō: Hokuseido Press, 1931.

An American Miscellany. 2 vols. Ed. Albert Mordell. New York: Dodd, Mead & Co., 1924.

Barbarous Barbers and Other Stories. Ed. Ichiro Nishizaki. Tōkyō: Hokuseido Press, 1939.

Children of the Levee. Ed. O. W. Frost. Intro. John Ball. Lexington, Ky.: University of Kentucky Press, 1957.

Chita: A Memory of Lost Island. New York: Harper & Bros., 1889.

Creole Sketches. Ed. Charles W. Hutson. Boston and New York: Houghton Mifflin Co., 1924.

The Crime of Sylvestre Bonnard. By Anatole France. New York: Harper & Bros., 1890.

Exotics and Retrospectives. Boston: Little, Brown & Co., 1898.

Fantastics and Other Fancies. Ed. Charles W. Hutson. Boston and New York: Houghton Mifflin Co., 1914.

Gleanings in Buddha-Fields. Boston and New York: Houghton Mifflin Co., 1897.

Glimpses of Unfamiliar Japan. 2 vols. Boston and New York: Houghton Mifflin Co., 1894.

In Ghostly Japan. Boston: Little, Brown & Co., 1899.

Japan: An Attempt at Interpretation. New York: Macmillan Co., 1904.

Japanese Fairy Tales. 5 vols. Tōkyō: Hasegawa, 1898–1922.

Japanese Lyrics. Boston and New York: Houghton Mifflin Co., 1915.

A Japanese Miscellany. Boston: Little, Brown & Co., 1901.

Karma. Ed. Albert Mordell. New York: Boni & Liveright, 1918.

Kokoro. Boston and New York: Houghton Mifflin Co., 1896.

Kottō. New York: Macmillan Co., 1902.

Kwaidan. Boston and New York: Houghton Mifflin Co., 1904.

Leaves from the Diary of an Impressionist. Ed. Ferris Greenslet. Boston and New York: Houghton Mifflin Co., 1911.

The Life and Letters of Lafcadio Hearn. 2 vols. Ed. Elizabeth Bisland. Boston and New York: Houghton Mifflin Co., 1906.

Occidental Gleanings. 2 vols. Ed. Albert Mordell. New York: Dodd, Mead & Co., 1925.

One of Cleopatra's Nights and Other Fantastic Romances. By Théophile Gautier. New York: R. Worthington, 1882.

Out of the East. Boston and New York: Houghton Mifflin Co., 1895.

The Romance of the Milky Way and Other Studies and Stories. Intro. Ferris Greenslet. Boston and New York: Houghton Mifflin Co., 1905.

Saint Anthony and Other Stories. By Guy de Maupassant. Ed. Albert Mordell. New York: Albert and Charles Boni, 1924.

The Selected Writings of Lafcadio Hearn. Ed. Henry Goodman. New York: The Citadel Press, 1949.

Selected Writings of Lafcadio Hearn. Ed. The Hearn Centennial Committee. Tōkyō: Kenkyusha, 1953.

Shadowings. Boston: Little, Brown & Co., 1900.

Sketches and Tales from the French. Ed. Albert Mordell. Tōkyō: Hokuseido Press, 1935.

Some Chinese Ghosts. Boston: Roberts Bros., 1887.

Some New Letters and Writings of Lafcadio Hearn. Ed. Sanki Ichikawa. Tōkyō: Kenkyusha, 1925.

Stories from Emile Zola. By Emile Zola. Ed. Albert Mordell. Tōkyō: Hokuseido Press, 1935.

Stories from Pierre Loti. By Pierre Loti. Ed. Albert Mordell. Tōkyō: Hokuseido Press, 1933.

Stray Leaves from Strange Literature. Boston: James R. Osgood & Co., 1884.

The Temptation of St. Anthony. By Gustave Flaubert. New York: Alice Harriman Co., 1911.

Two Years in the French West Indies. New York: Harper & Bros., 1890.

The Writings of Lafcadio Hearn. Koizumi Edition. 16 vols. Boston: Houghton Mifflin Co., 1922.

Youma. New York: Harper & Bros., 1890.

SECONDARY SOURCES

BISLAND, ELIZABETH. See *Life and Letters,* under Works. Also contained in *Writings,* Vols. XIII–XVI. Basic biographical information from a close friend.

COWLEY, MALCOLM. "Lafcadio Hearn," Introduction to *The Selected Writings of Lafcadio Hearn,* ed. Henry Goodman. New York: Citadel Press, 1949. The first important study from a critical point of view; still extremely illuminating.

FROST, O. W. *Young Hearn.* Tōkyō: Hokuseido Press, 1958. Painstaking research on the obscure earlier years; sloppily printed.

HUNEKER, JAMES. *Ivory, Apes and Peacocks.* New York: Charles Scribner's Sons, 1915. View of Hearn by a contemporary American writer.

KENNARD, NINA. *Lafcadio Hearn.* New York: D. Appleton & Co., 1912. Basic biographical information.

KOIZUMI, KAZUO. *Father and I.* Boston and New York: Houghton Mifflin Co., 1935. Recollections by Hearn's eldest son.

KOIZUMI, SETSUKO. *Reminiscences of Lafcadio Hearn.* Boston and New York: Houghton Mifflin Co., 1918. By his wife; quaint.

MINER, EARL. *The Japanese Tradition in British and American Literature.* Princeton: Princeton University Press, 1958. Important sections on Hearn's literary position and influences.

MORDELL, ALBERT. See the Introductions to *An American Miscellany, Occidental Gleanings,* and *Saint Anthony* in Works. Helpful critical principles and stylistic analysis.

———. *Discoveries: Essays on Lafcadio Hearn.* Tōkyō: Orient/West, 1964. Collection of the scholarship by the grand old man of Hearn criticism.

PERKINS, P. D. and IONE. *Lafcadio Hearn: A Bibliography of His Writings.* Intro. Sanki Ichikawa. Boston: Houghton Mifflin Co., 1934. *The* Hearn bibliography.

ROBERT, MARCEL. *Lafcadio Hearn.* 2 vols. Tōkyō: Hokuseido Press, 1950–51. Not only a sensitive psychological study, but contains the best literary analysis of Hearn's writings. Ends with 1897, however.

STEVENSON, ELIZABETH. *Lafcadio Hearn.* New York: Macmillan Co., 1961. A model biography, certainly the best on Hearn. Excellent notes and references.

TINKER, EDWARD L. *Lafcadio Hearn's American Days.* New York: Dodd, Mead & Co., 1924. Important biographical information and a few uncollected works.

Toyama University Library. *Descriptive Catalogue of the Hearniana in the Hearn Library of the Toyama University.* Toyama, Japan, 1959. The excellence of the collection at Toyama is such that this catalogue constitutes a companion bibliography to Perkins. Especially good on books and articles on Hearn in Japanese.

YU, BEONGCHEON. *An Ape of Gods: The Art and Thought of Lafcadio Hearn.* Detroit: Wayne State University Press, 1964. The first complete study of Hearn's philosophy and literary criticism; literary work from the point of view of themes and ideas.

Index

Entries are repeated except where an item is discussed continuously for several pages. Thus, the reader may use the index to estimate the relative importance of a certain item in the works of Hearn.

Akinari [Ueda Akinari], 110–113, 135

Ball, John, 137
Baudelaire, Charles, 24, 54, 131
Bisland, Elizabeth, 137, 138

Canada, 9, 70, 80–82
Cincinnati, 5, 8, 11–36, 84, 92, 97, 99, 124, 126–127
Cincinnati Commercial, 8, 14–15, 16–22, 37–41, 129, 131
Cincinnati Enquirer, 8, 11–16, 129
Coppée François, 30, 32–33, 131
Cowley, Malcolm, 136, 138

Daudet, Alphonse, 23–24, 30, 32, 34, 131
Dickens, Charles, 79
Dorson, R. M., 133, 133–134
Dostoevski, Fyodr, 130

Faulkner, William, 136
Flaubert, Gustave, 23, 27–29, 34, 130, 138
Florida, 9, 61–62
France, 8, 124
France, Anatole, 29–30, 137
Frost, O. W., 5, 18, 132, 137, 138

Gautier, Théophile, 23, 25–27, 54, 130, 138
Goodman, Henry, 138, 138
Greenslet, Ferris, 137, 138

Harper's Magazine, 133
Hearn, Lafcadio
and dreams, 13–14, 46, 48, 50–51, 60, 62–64, 79, 91, 108–109, 110, 114, 115, 118–119, 119–122, 122, 125
and lyric poetry, 40–41, 45–46, 96, 96, 99, 102–107, 115, 124, 134, 137
and punctuation, 15–16, 23
autobiography, 13–14, 55, 62–64, 80, 119–123, 124, 135
chronology, 8–9
essays and speculative writings, 6, 62–63, 84, 89–90, 90–91, 91–92, 93, 95, 99, 107–108, 123
fictional prose narratives, 15, 17, 22, 23–24, 25–36, 37–38, 43, 44–45, 46–54, 55–58, 58–61, 62–64, 64–69, 74, 76–78, 78–79, 79–80, 88–89, 89, 91, 91–92, 93, 94–95, 95, 96, 108–119, 122–124, 125, 126–127, 135
ghost stories, 14, 19, 26–27, 27, 27, 47, 48–49, 49–50, 64, 73–74, 74, 85, 89, 89, 89, 96, 108–109, 109, 109–110, 110–112, 114, 114, 114, 115, 115–116, 116–117, 117, 117–118, 118, 118, 119, 120–121, 126–127, 135
insect writings, 62, 63, 64, 75–76, 102–107, 124, 134
news reporting, 11–14, 15–16, 17–19, 19–22, 23, 37–38, 92–93, 108, 123
on Negroes, 14, 14–15, 18–19, 41–46, 70, 71–72, 73, 74, 76–78, 78–79, 84
TRANSLATION
gen., 6, 23–25, 28, 30, 33, 102–103, 108–109, 127
from French, 23–24, 24–36, 108, 127

retranslation, 55, 58–59, 134
from Japanese, 96–97, 100, 102–
107, 107–119, 126–127, 134, 134
TRANSLATIONS, BY AUTHOR
Akinari [Ueda Akinari], 110–
113
Charles Baudelaire, 24
François Coppée, 30, 32–33
Alphonse Daudet, 23–24, 30,
32, 34
Gustave Flaubert, 23, 27–29, 34
Anatole France, 9, 29–30
Théophile Gautier, 8, 23, 25–27
Pierre Loti, 23, 33
Guy de Maupassant, 23, 30, 30–
32
Octave Mirbeau, 36
Gérard de Nerval, 24
Auguste Villiers de l'Isle Adam,
24, 34–36, 108
Emile Zola, 23, 33, 108
travel sketches and descriptive
pieces, 16–18, 18–19, 38–41, 41–
46, 61–62, 70–72, 74–76, 78,
80–82, 83–84, 84–89, 90–91,
92–94, 97, 99–102, 119–120,
122, 127
use of world literature, 54–55, 58–
59, 126
WORKS OF:
The Adventures of Walter
Schnaffs [Maupassant], 131, 137
"After the War," 92
"All in White," 47–48
"Almost a Riot," 12–13
An American Miscellany, 129,
132–133, 137, 139
"L'Amour Apres La Mort," 49–
50
"Ants," 134
"Arria Marcella" [Gautier], 27
"At a Railway Station," 92
"At Hinomisaki," 86
"At Mionoseki," 85, 87–88, 89
"At the Gate of the Tropics,"
39–40
"At the Market of the Dead,"
85–86
"At Yaidzu," 122

"Autheman's Suicide" [Daudet],
34
"Banjo Jim's Story," 19
"Barbarous Barbers," 14
Barbarous Barbers and Other
Stories, 129–130, 131–132, 137
"Bête-ni-pié," 75–76
"The Bird Wife," 57
"Bits of Life and Death," 91
"Bits of Poetry," 103, 134
"Black Varieties," 18–19
"The Blessed Bread" [Coppée],
32
"Buddhist Allusions in Japan-
ese Folk-Song," 96–97
"Butterflies," 134
Buying Christmas Toys and
Other Essays, 132
"By the Japanese Sea," 89
"The Case of O-Dai," 123
"The Cedar Closet," 14
"Char-Coal," 45–46
"The Chief City of the Province
of the Gods," 86, 89
"A Child of the Levee," 19
Children of the Levee, 18–19,
137
Chita, 9, 17, 64–69, 127, 132,
137
"Clarimonde" [Gautier], 26–27
"The Corpse-Rider," 116–117
"The Schnaffs Character," 43–44
"A Creole Journal," 43
Creole Sketches, 41–46, 131–
132, 137
The Crime of Sylvestre Bon-
nard [Anatole France], 29–30,
137
"The Crucified Lions" [Flau-
bert], 34
"The Curé of Cucugnan" [Dau-
det], 32
"A Dead Love," 49–50
"A Dead Secret," 135
"Denis" [Maupassant], 31
"Diplomacy," 118
"Dolly—An Idyl of the Levee,"
19
"La Douane," 42

"The Dowry" [Maupassant], 30

"Dragon-Flies," 104–105, 134, 134

"The Dream of a Summer Day," 91

"The Dream of Akinosuké," 118

"The Eater of Dreams," 119

Editorials, 132

"Ephemerae"
See *Leaves from the Diary of an Impressionist*

"The Eternal Feminine," 91

Exotics and Retrospectives, 9, 99–102, 102, 105, 120, 122, 134–135, 137

Fantastics and Other Fancies, 46–54, 115, 132, 137

"Fireflies," 104, 134

"The Fountain Maiden," 57

Fragments from the *Kalevala,* 58

"Frogs," 105, 134

"From a Traveling Diary," 94

"From Hōki to Oki," 86–87

"From the Diary of an English Teacher," 86

"Fuji-no-Yama," 99–102

"Furisodé," 109

"Gaki," 107, 134

"The Genius of Japanese Civilization," 94

"The Ghostly Kiss," 48–49

"Gibbeted," 19–22, 30

Gleanings in Buddha-Fields, 9, 83, 95–98, 137

"A Glimpse of Tendencies," 92, 93

Glimpses of Unfamiliar Japan, 9, 83, 84–89, 137

"Goblin Poetry," 134

"Gothic Horror," 120

"Grande Anse," 73

"La Guiablesse," 73, 74

"Haru," 94–95

"Heiké-Gani," 134

"Hi-Mawari," 135

"The Idyl of a French Snuff-Box," 51–52

"In a Cup of Tea," 118

"Incense," 122

In Ghostly Japan, 9, 102, 103, 109, 109–110, 115, 115, 122, 122, 122–123, 134–136, 137

"Ingwa-Banashi," 115

"Insect Musicians," 134

"Insect Studies," 134

"In the Cave of the Children's Ghosts," 85

"In the Twilight of the Gods," 93

"The Invitation to Sleep" [Coppée], 32–33

Japan: An Attempt at Interpretation, 9, 107–108, 137

Japanese Fairy Tales, 137

Japanese Lyrics, 137

A Japanese Miscellany, 9, 102, 104–105, 106, 110–112, 112–113, 114, 117, 123, 123–124, 134–136, 137

"The Japanese Smile," 84

"Jiujutsu," 91

"Jiu-Roku-Zakura," 135

"Jizō," 85

"John Algernon Owen," 12

Karma, 9, 132, 133, 137

"Karma," 79–80

"Kimiko," 94

"King Candaules" [Gautier], 27

"Kitsune," 88–89

"Kitzuki: The Most Ancient Shrine of Japan," 86

Kokoro, 9, 91–95, 137

Kottō, 9, 102, 104, 107, 109, 115, 118, 124, 134–136, 137

"Kusa-Hibari," 124

Kwaidan, 9, 102, 108, 114, 115, 117–118, 118, 118, 118, 134–135, 137

Leaves from the Diary of an Impressionist, 61–62, 137

"Legend of Tchi-Niu," 59–60

"The Legend of the Monster Misfortune," 57

"A Letter from Japan," 108

"Levee Life," 18

"Levitation," 120

The Life and Letters of, 121, 136, 137, 138

"The Little Red Kitten," 46

"A Living God," 95
Lys, 70, 78
"A Madman" [Maupassant], 31
"Martinique Sketches," 70, 72–79
"M D C C C L I I I," 52–53
"Memphis to Orleans," 38–39
"A Mephistophelian," 53–54
"A Midsummer Trip to the Tropics," 70–72
"Mr. Handy's Life," 14
"Mosquitoes," 107, 134
"Mujina," 118
"The Mummy's Foot" [Gautier], 130
"My First Day in the Orient," 84–85
"My First Romance," 121
"My Guardian Angel," 121
"Natalika," 57–58
"New Orleans in Wet Weather," 40–41
The New Radiance and Other Scientific Sketches, 132
"Nightmare Touch," 120, 120–121
"Ningyō-no-Haka," 96
"Notes of a Trip to Kyōto," 97
"Notes on Forrest's Funeral," 37, 38, 44, 122, 133
"The Nun of the Temple of Amida," 94
Occidental Gleanings, 129, 131–132, 138, 139
"Of a Promise Broken," 117
"Of a Promise Kept," 110–112
"Of Ghosts and Goblins," 89
"Old Japanese Songs," 106, 134
"The Old Man" [Maupassant], 31
"Omphale" [Gautier], 27
"On a Bridge," 123–124
One of Cleopatra's Nights [Gautier], 25–27, 138
"One of Cleopatra's Nights" [Gautier], 25–26, 130
"The One Pill-Box," 50–51
"Oshidori," 135
Out of the East, 9, 89–91, 138
"Out of the Street," 96

"Ozias Midwinter Letters," 38–41, 131
" 'Pa Combiné, Chè!' " 70, 76–78
"Pariah People," 18
"A Parricide" [Maupassant], 30
"A Passional Karma," 109–110
"La Pelée," 74–75
"The Phalanx in Battle" [Flaubert], 34
"A Pilgrimage to Enoshima," 85
"Porcelain Painting," 16–17, 133
"Les Porteuses," 73
"Pundari," 57
"Rabbi Yochanan ben Zachai," 57
" 'Rags, Iron, Stoves!' " 17
"Recollections of the Franco-Prussian War" [Mirbeau], 36
"The Reconciliation," 115–116
"The Red Bridal," 91
"Un Revenant," 73, 73–74, 122
"Riki-Baka," 135
"Rokuro-Kubi," 135
The Romance of the Milky Way, 9, 102, 105, 108, 119, 119–120, 134–135, 138
"The Romance of the Milky Way," 105, 134
"The Sacrifice: Moloch The Devourer" [Flaubert], 34
"Saint Anthony" [Maupassant], 31
St. Anthony and Other Stories [Maupassant], 30–31, 131, 138, 139
"The Screen Maiden," 114
"The Secret of the Scaffold" [Villiers de l'Isle Adam], 34–36
The Selected Writings of Lafcadio Hearn, 129, 132–136, 138
Selected Writings of Lafcadio Hearn [Kenkyūsha], 138
"Sémi," 105, 105–106, 134
Shadowings, 9, 102, 105, 105–106, 106, 114, 114, 115, 115, 115–116, 116–117, 120–121, 134–135, 138
"Shinjū," 88

Sketches and Tales from the French, 32–33, 34–36, 130–131, 138
"Slow Starvation," 13
Some Chinese Ghosts, 8, 58–61, 138
Some New Letters and Writings, 138
"Some Pictures of Poverty," 17–18
"Some Positive Opinions," 44–45, 54
"Songs of Japanese Children," 106, 134
"Steeple Climbers," 14, 99
"The Stone Buddha," 91
Stories from Emile Zola, 32, 131, 138
Stories from Pierre Loti, 32, 131, 138
"The Story of Aoyagi," 135
"The Story of a Pheasant," 135
"Story of a Slave," 14–15
"The Story of Itō Norisuké," 119
"The Story of Kōgi the Priest," 112–113
"The Story of Kwashin Koji," 114
"The Story of Mimi-Nashi-Hōichi," 117–118
"Story of O-Kamé," 109
"The Story of O-Tei," 135
"Stranger than Fiction," 119–120
Stray Leaves from Strange Literature, 8, 54–58, 138
"The Sympathy of Benten," 114
"The Tale of the Porcelain God," 60–61
Talks to Writers, 134
The Temptation of Saint Anthony [Flaubert], 28–29, 138
"Three Dreams," 62–64
Three Popular Ballads, 133
" 'Ti Canotié,' " 132
"Torn Letters," 132
"To the Fountain of Youth," 61–62
"The Tradition of the Tea-Plant," 60

"Two Actors for One Role" [Gautier], 130
Two Years in the French West Indies, 9, 70–79, 83, 138
"Ubazakura," 135
"Ululation," 122–123
"Vespertina Cognitio," 120, 122
"Violent Cremation," 15–16
"The Vision of the Dead Creole," 47
"Voices of Dawn," 46
"Vultur Aura," 62
"A Walk" [Maupassant], 30–31
"Why Crabs are Boiled Alive," 42–43
"A Winter Journey to Japan," 70, 80–82
"A Wish Fulfilled," 91
"With Kyūshū Students," 90
Writings: Koizumi Ed., 131–132, 132–136, 138
"Yamaraja," 57
Youma, 9, 70, 78–79, 138
"Yuki-Onna," 135

Hemingway, Ernest, 123
Huneker, James, 138–139
Hutson, Charles W., 132, 137, 137

Ichikawa, Sanki, 138

Japan
  general, 5, 9, 14, 83–119, 122, 123–124, 124, 126–127
  Kōbe, 9, 98
  Kumamoto, 9, 83, 90, 98
  Matsue and Izumo province, 9, 83, 85, 86–89, 90, 98
  Mt. Fuji, 14, 99–102
  Tōkyō, 9, 98
  Yokohama, 9, 84–85

Keene, Donald, 127
Kennard, Nina, 139
Koizumi, Kazuo, 139
Koizumi, Setsuko, 9, 83, 108, 139
Koizumi, Yakumo
  See Hearn, Lafcadio

Lemaître, Jules, 131
Lippincott's Magazine, 133
Loti, Pierre, 23, 33, 131
.
Manzoni, Alessandro, 79
Maupassant, Guy de, 23, 30, 30–
    32, 109, 131, 137, 137
Michaud, Régis, 130
Miner, Earl, 127, 134, 136, 139
Mirbeau, Octave, 36, 131
Mordell, Albert, 5, 134, 136, 137,
    137, 138, 138, 138, 138, 138,
    139, 139
Morris, Ivan, 127

Nerval, Gérard de, 24
New Orleans and Louisiana, 8, 37–
    46, 46, 61, 64–69, 83, 97, 98,
    119, 124, 126–127
New Orleans Item, 8
New Orleans Times-Democrat, 8
New York, 8, 94
Nishizaki, Ichirō, 137

Perkins, Ione, 139
Perkins, P. D., 139
Poe, E. A., 14, 20, 54, 115, 136

Robert, Marcel, 5, 24, 130, 130, 130,
    133, 139

Seidensticker, Edward, 127
Seki, Keigo, 133, 133
Stevenson, Elizabeth, 5, 131, 134,
    136, 139

Tinker, Edward L., 132, 139
Tōkyō University, 9
Toyama University Library, 139
Turgenev, Ivan, 130

Verhaeren, Emile, 115
Villiers de l'Isle Adam, Auguste, 24,
    34–36, 108, 131

Waseda University, 9
West Indies, 9, 70–79, 79–80, 84,
    119–120, 124, 126–127
    Martinique, 9, 14, 70–71, 72–79,
        79–80, 83, 92, 97, 120
    Mount Pelée, 14, 74–75, 99

Yu, Beongcheon, 5, 135, 136, 139

Zola, Emile, 23, 33, 108, 131